Y0-DWL-671

Will America Accept Love at Halftime?

Will America Accept

Love at Halftime?

(Or how to survive Pro-Football Sunday)

By **JIM KLOBUCHAR**

Cartoons by Jerry Fearing

Ross & Haines, Inc.
Minneapolis, Minnesota   55408
1972

ISBN 0-87018-066-5

Copyright A September 1972 by Ross & Haines, Inc., Minneapolis, Minnesota 55408. Copyright under International and Pan-American Conventions. All rights reserved, including the rights to reproduce this book, or portions thereof, in any form, except for the inclusion of brief quotations in any type review. This book was printed by Bolger Publications/Creative Printing, 428 North Washington, Minneapolis, Minnesota 55401.

All inquiries should be addressed to Mark Zelenovich, Inc., Minneapolis, Minnesota 55402. 612-336-5891.

This is for my wife,
who never asks what is a rotating zone or a
Gap 8, not in ignorance but more in kindness.

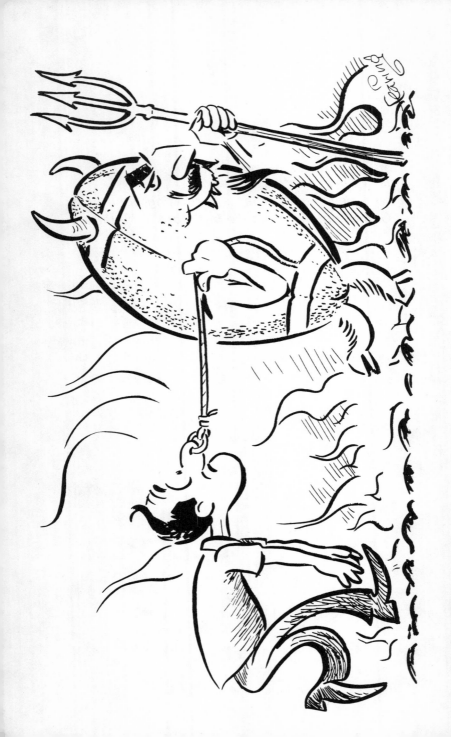

Foreward

Some fundamentalist ministers are convinced pro football is the creation of the devil, and there are some seething housewives who do not necessarily disagree.

The ministers contend pro football is cutting into time the penitents would normally spend being contrite for their sins. I know housewives who maintain that all the contrition in the world isn't enough to absolve their ogling husbands of the worst sin of all — six hours in front of a television set on Sunday afternoon.

Plainly, these views are not unanimously held.

Football watching, both in the arena and living room, has by now graduated into a genuine cultural form. It stands beside working, church-going, committe-organizing and lovemaking as an important pursuit of the masses. Troubles occur when it conflicts with one or several of these.

That, in part, was what provoked this informal manual on how the average American citizen can get through the football season without destroying the institution of marriage or the sanity of the various family members.

It may not tell you all you need to know about pro football watching. But it should tell you enough to stalemate a wiseguy neighbor, to improve your sex life on Sunday or to get through the weekend without corroding your digestive tract.

It is offered impartially to men and women, largely on the theory that the family which yells together jells together. I do not offer myself as an expert necessarily but merely as a survivor. For five years I viewed the spectacle — the quilted and booted pilgrims in the stands, the masked gargantuans on the field — from the distant safety of the newspaper press box. In later years I reformed and consigned my cold nose and related body members to the gales and the cloudbursts.

To be a truly well-adjusted fan in the second deck, I discovered, requires special qualities of craftiness, stamina and a fast hand for a proferred thermos. Not all qualify. What follows here is a kind of handbook for all who have been touched by the football delirium, willingly, accidentally or against their better judgment.

I will put out only one disclaimer. I am not personally responsible for any of the techniques or measures herein suggested, especially the ones for neglected housewives on how to counteract the Sunday celibacy of their husbands.

What do you want? A warranty?

Jim Klobuchar

July, 1972

Table of Contents

Amour Vs. a 405-Piece Band

The testament you're about to read is absolutely true.

Only the color of the witness' hair has been changed, to give her some merciful concealment from the neighbors.

She wrote to me, a newspaper columnist and reformed football writer, a man accustomed to the role of dartboard for the wounded derelicts of society.

She wrote with a cold, betrayed fury. You could see her as a Maid Marian who had just discovered that Robin Hood preferred shagging after the king's boars to tumbling with her in the thicket.

"I don't hate football," she said. "I don't even dislike it. I go to all the games. I humor my husband's drunken friends in the parking lot when one of them yells, 'hey, blondie, let's work on our bump-and-run.'

"I wear those goofie wool tassel caps and sneer when somebody mentions Howard Cosell. I pretend I know the difference between blitz and banana route — all the orthodox things like that.

"But the television is breaking me down. I'm not thinking about the divorce courts. I think of

1

the convents. I visualize myself as an abbess. It's what football television is making me. And I don't have that much virtue.

"Years ago we used to go see the college games on Saturday afternoon, five or six times a year. We made it a blowout. We had a big Friday night party at one of the supper clubs, then the university game Saturday afternoon and then a nice, intimate, conjugal withdrawal period Saturday night.

"My husband's qualities as a bed partner on those weekends were the same ones you always associate with a champion, and I used to tell him so. I'm talking about things like versatility, resourcefulness and comeback ability.

"TV football and the pros have turned it all around. Our Saturday nights now are what the Friday nights used to be, the big party night. Only now he parties like a big wheel because he knows so much about the game from TV that he feels like one of the owners. The team is right in the living room, all the time, and he spends the whole party with our friends and neighbors talking about our front four and how some guy has got to have the world's fastest release. It goes on that way for hours. By the time it's over he's all smashed out and worthless for anything but dead ballast.

"I could roll with that, I suppose, except that Sunday football on television doesn't start when it used to. He used to turn the set on at 1 o'clock. He would watch the ball game, turn it off when the game was over and we had the rest of the day for walks, candlelight and various parlor games.

"I'll tell you what it's come to.

"There were some Sunday mornings a few years ago when I could drag him to church. That was before the university football coach started coming on at 11 Sunday morning.

"For a couple of years the Minnesota coach, Murray Warmath, would tell us all about the big Saturday game. My husband is kind of fuzzy about college football now but he spent his Army training in the South and Murray Warmath's drawl used to remind him of peach trees, magnolias and God knows what else.

"So Murray came on with the highlights of the Saturday afternoon football game at something like 10:30 or 11 in the morning on Sunday instead of the middle of the afternoon, because pro football is going wide open all afternoon. Even if there's time on that channel in the afternoon the college highlights would get chewed up by the other station because NBC has the AFL doubleheaders spread out from noon until George Blanda kicks his field goal at 1 minute to 6.

"Along about the middle of the college game clips Sunday morning my husband starts getting psyched up just thinking about the Vikings-Lions game. To relieve the pressure he goes into the kitchen and makes himself a screwdriver.

"He used to drink Bloody Marys but he has decided now that Worcestershire sauce is a corruptive influence on good gin.

"By noon he's got all of the TV lineups from the Sunday sports page spread out on the coffee table.

"It's not a minute too soon, either, because this Al Derogatis is coming in on the tube telling us what to look for when Kansas City lines up with its tight end in the eye instead of the slot. Al says this confuses the strong safety.

"Isn't that beautiful? The strong safety is confused. What about me? Am I supposed to be panting to find out where the tight end lines up? In spite of this, the camera zooms in on the tight end. The only thing I notice is that he's wearing form-fit pants, and if I were the tight end I would never line up in a crouch like that.

"So now they've got some kind of preview or countdown or something. My husband looks on this now as his hors d'ouevres. He takes it in like miniwieners before the steak. We talked about that once and the idea of the AFL noon special as an appetizer impressed him so much that he went into the kitchen and made himself another screwdriver.

"That's how the afternoon gets started. At halftime of the AFL noon special he switches channels for the Viking countdown. All these countdowns leave me unlit. They spend the first five minutes showing football players with orange and fuchsia faces doing some tribal dance, trying to stay up with an orchestration that sounds like Henry Mancini doodling on a bad trip.

"Then we get the torn ticket bit for a little while. Some bank comes on and tells us to get your kicks today kids but don't forget to invest in tomorrow.

"They put on some highlights which I have seen a few dozen times before. Carl Eller is telling the interviewer all about pride and how much the players enjoy the camaraderie and manly satisfactions of pro football. He also almost, but not quite, mentions the 50 grand.

"They put on the orange faces and torn tickets again at the end of the show. Like I say, it doesn't get me into convulsions but my husband reacts like Pavlov's dog when they tinkle the bell. He's got his collar open and the audio up and his shirt-tails down. You just know this is going to be one of those games where the ballplayers are going to run through walls and barbed wire.

"If you have any doubts, Tom Brookshier, the color announcer, reminds us about it four different times between the national anthem and the kickoff.

"If the wind blows the football off the kickoff tee, Brookshier will remind us the fifth time.

"My husband goes through all of the predictable agonies and euphorias for three hours. I am conditioned to it. I don't begrudge it. I get excited myself, especially in the last two minutes of each half when they play most of the game.

"But when the Viking game is over you ought to bear in mind that since 11 o'clock my husband has had his nose in the television watching seven hours of football, with the exception of a few minutes around noon when he shaved and laid some beer in the refrigerator.

"In the normal course of things you would expect the world around us to begin intruding after seven hours of football television. Real Life makes a comeback. Are the Oakland Raiders vs. the Denver Broncos real life? Is George Blanda real life? The trouble is you have to wait until 1 minute to 6 to find out.

"Okay, my husband is no different than millions of other men. The trouble is I'm no different than millions of other women. What have you got in the way of a soulmate after seven hours of football? A dangling shirttail, a soft belly, tired eyeballs and a bitter feeling toward the corner linebacker.

"That may not be bad for an epitaph but it's not much for scorching amour.

"I hear the argument that a woman ought to be happy the man is under roof all that time.

"I'm unhappy because 6 o'clock isn't the end of it. He's still got the replays left on the 6 and 10 o'clock news shows, and two years ago he used to stay up waiting for the Bud Grant Show at 10:30. I watched it once and mistook the scene for the station's test pattern.

"What I'm saying is that as far as his love-making powers go, after all that football my husband has reached the point of emotional and physical exhaustion by Sunday night and has become a living, wheezing turnover."

No more devastating judgment can be pronounced on the American male.

A turnover; an anonymous digit in the scoring

summary.

Is the lady an isolated victim of the Sunday afternoon malaise, or does she have hundreds of thousands of distressed sisters who trace their current sex troubles to televised pro football?

No accurate statistics are available. But there is no exaggerating the steady burn of this lady's indignation.

Only a heartless klutz would have ignored her. I telephoned.

"You are feeling neglected because of televised football?" I asked.

"Typhoid Mary has had better years," she said. "In a word, I am not getting a whole lot."

"Have you thought," I said with a great surge of delicacy, "about trying to entice your husband at halftime?"

"I have," she said icily. "But the sonofabitch likes bands, too."

I hung up, twitching sympathetically, but with some sense of guilt. We may very well be approaching a social crisis in this country and who among us can afford to fling the first stone. I called on one of the ranking marriage counselors in the community, Dr. John Eichenlaub.

"You get an awful lot of mumbo-jumbo about what happens to the typical male watching football," the sage replied. "I don't think there's any doubt about football giving him an identification. Your typical fan might be saying to himself 'kill,' while he's riding on Carl Eller's shoulders. And when Eller bangs his shoulder into somebody's gut the fan feels a degree of relief just as if he has been able to do it himself.

"There's a great psychological outlet being involved with a team or a star player. So he feels proud and exuberant when the team wins, and he feels betrayed and humiliated when it loses.

"Whatever happens, he buries himself in the game and nothing the woman can do intellectually or physically is really going to distract him. The reason for that is that his ego is either in the wringer or bathing in the sun on every play, depending on how it goes.

"Now, of course, this is the kind of involvement the woman is trying to get out of her marriage. So even if she tries to get interested in the game for defensive reasons she usually feels either a little bit of jealousy or plain resentment that these jock-strapped hulks are getting the kind of hypnotic attention that only she used to be able to get out of her husband.

"The net effect may well be to convince the woman she isn't getting enough of what matters.

"People ask if it's true that more and more women are watching pro football because they have made the players their own sex objects? No, I doubt that's the reason. Despite the form-fit pants, there's nothing particularly sexy about a guy who wears a helmet, face guard, five pounds of gauze and half the mud of the East River.

"There is one thing that many women do identify

with in the football player, though. Women are becoming increasingly aggressive in our society. So they look on the aggressive football player not so much as a sex object but as a kind of extension of their own personality and ambitions.

"As to the effects of seven hours of football watching on the male's sexual prowess, I think these observations can be made: Under certain conditions the excitement of an athletic contest can stimulate a person erotically; that is, to provide him with an outlet for this excitement. As a rule, however, a man is more likely to be plain bushed than dramatically horny after a half-day of watching football.

"The trouble is, people react in different ways sexually to periods of excitement. You have some who feel a build-up in urges, but more of them probably have a letdown period — of the kind the woman is railing about here. In such cases a sexual act after an emotional experience in a football game is probably going to be unsatisfactory.

"With some men, it's certainly true that their preoccupation with football lessens their concentration on things like sex and makes them ineffective partners to that extent. You can compare it with a gung-ho salesman. If he is on the verge of making a sale, his pulse may go way up and the adrenalin is flowing and nothing else around him really interests him.

"He's thinking only about his business. In the bedroom he's probably a mechanical man and he may need some oiling at that. But you take his mind away from his business, and his sex pace goes up triple. The same will hold true in many cases of men whose excitement is centered on football."

All this tells me is that if Sigmund Freud had gone to Notre Dame instead of Oedipus Institute, the world would be a happier place and certainly a saner one today.

The point is that women who imagine their sex lives blighted by the football hysteria are ignoring the first precept of the good competitor: "Remember, they all put on their pants one leg at a time."

There is no reason for the American housewife of today to go unrequited or untended.

The apple, after all, was nothing more than the first recorded use of the trick offense.

To put the old thrills of the hammock back into Sunday and Monday, consider these contingency plans. They have been distilled from many frank suggestions offered to the agony columnists by women ranging from the very thoughtful to the very predatory:

1. Have a tryst while waiting for the bands to form at halftime.

For all but the most methodical, this is an entirely satisfactory interlude. It is especially true during Dallas Cowboy games when the 405-piece bands and pom-pon girls from Texas A&I or Prairie View require extra time and large staging areas.

Admitted, there are some band-conscious dudes

who might feel impoverished to miss the first few minutes of the intermission show. These can be soothed by the resourceful housewife who entertains her husband at breakfast with band music from the record player. To cover all halftime possibilities, three records are especially recommended: America's Favorite Marches, Al Hirt Plays Beethoven, and Hail to the Chief, the latter a musical tribute that has been used interchangeably in the last four years for Richard Nixon and Pete Rozelle.

No erotic exertion is recommended for halftime of games televised from Los Angeles and New Orleans. The usual intermission show in Los Angeles is to send a man rocketing into space. This might be a distraction and possibly a bad omen for halftime liaison at home. At New Orleans roughly the same kind of production is achieved through the use of manned hot air balloons, some of which puncture. The symbolism for halftime romancers can be shattering.

2. **During the Marlboro commercial.** For some, this may have the handicap of thin time tolerances. There is a danger, for example, that you might miss at least the first play when they go back to live action. However, make note of the down and distance before the commercial starts. From this, knowledgeable fans may very soundly predict the kind of play the quarterback will call on the first snap after the cowboy rides off for the mesa, billowing smoke.

If it is second and seven when the commercial comes on, you can pretty well count on a pass play. This means the quarterback will customarily take longer to call the play in the huddle. Details like this are important. Under the circumstances, they could be critical.

On the other hand, if he calls a draw play you may be out of luck.

3. During the two-minute offense. There are both benefits and debits here. This is the sequence at the end of the first half and the fourth quarter after the two-minute warning has been given. The action is likely to be thrilling here and may even be, as one color announcer described it, immemorable. On the other hand, the two-minute offenses usually average 25 minutes, a span that certainly will be agreeable to all interests and should remove any need for hasty, slap-dash nestling.

4. During Tom Brookshier's explanation of a complicated play. A bonus here for the impetuous. Brookshier usually begins by outlining what happened. He then outlines what he thinks might have happened and then what should have happened. After this he gives you the applicable rule, which he often misquotes. The explanation must then be extended while the play-by-play man explains what he thought Brookshier meant, as opposed to what he said. By the time they finish they are into the Marlboro commercial, so this is one of those rare double-headers the savvy lover will watch for.

5. While Francis Tarkenton is looking for a receiver. This is particularly recommended for suspense-lovers. Time here is variable. First tested by a housewife in the Minneapolis suburb of Robbinsdale, who cowed her husband by going onto the offensive when Tarkenton started a scramble against the Bears in 1963. She hit the off button on the TV with the announcement: "It's okay, he'll be back that way five more times before he goes out of bounds."

"We never," she disclosed sweetly, "missed a play."

Don't Let Them Run the Banana

At one time English was the odds-on favorite in America's search for a national language.

It has since undergone a succession of setbacks, the latest being teen-agers, and has now been largely replaced by footballese as the most widely spoken tongue in the republic.

Among the world's great languages only Italian is spoken with more ardor than Pro Football and only Hebrew wreaks more befuddlement on the unwary bystander.

Novices among pro football watchers are often demoralized by what seems to them the easy brilliance and effortless genius with which seasoned fans talk the language.

Let me lay the myth right now that it takes years of struggling apprenticeship to be able to sit down in front of a television set, or behind a pillar at the ballpark, and to talk EXACTLY LIKE KYLE ROTE TALKS.

If it is any consolation to the timid greenhorn, be assured that the nation's living rooms are filled with millions of earnest quacks. Most of them manage to conceal their condition behind dazzling verbiage. This is borrowed in part from the color analyst, partly from this week's cover story in Sports Illustrated and the rest from the back of the Wheaties' box.

There is no evidence that saturation television and a glut of locker room literature, whose authors range from Joe Namath to Mrs. Francis Tarkenton, has changed our basic ignorance about what happens after the quarterback goes hut-hut.

Society recognizes that the line between what is expert and what merely sounds expert is fine and sometimes invisible. We honor both equally.

Okay, observe the neighbor settling in for the afternoon siege. You walk in and ask what's going on.

"The first time they got the ball they led off with a wedge and then tried a banana pattern," he replies.

"What are they doing?" you ask archly, "going for a first down or growing a garden?"

The neighbor exhales laboriously. "All right, if we have to we can go back to the sandbox. On first down the Lions sent the fullback straight up the middle with straightahead power blocking and on second down they sent the flanker down deep on long arching pattern that some of the pros call a banana but the more sophisticated ones call a cucumber."

"I'm glad for the flanker's sake they don't run a muskmellon," you observe. "It would be hard for the quarterback to snap off that kind of call in the huddle without stuttering. What do you think they'll try on third down?"

"It's fundamental. The Lions are looking at third and long. They got Farr in there but you figure after all those injuries he has lost a step, right? They got Owens in there, too, but it's third and nine and you just got to figure pass, with Landry probably going to the tight end Sanders."

"How do you figure that?"

"The Vikings are in a zone defense."

"How do you know that?"

"Don't you ever watch the Bud Grant Show? Without fail Bud Grant opens each show by saying, "as you know, most of the time we play zone defense . . . ""

"But sitting here right now in the living room, how do you recognize that the Vikings are going to be in a zone defense on third and long?"

"Are you calling Pat Summerall a liar? Are you some kind of loony? If the Vikings didn't line up in a zone defense the whole structure of pro football would be shaken and there would be a blue ribbon commission set up to get to the bottom of it."

"Why wouldn't the Lions' Landry throw a long pass against the zone?" you persist.

"Oh, my god, what do you do with your nights off? The reason you don't throw deep against the zone is that by the time the receiver gets down that far there's a safety man coming over to help the corner back and you got what amounts to double coverage on the deep receiver."

"So how do you attack the zone?"

"You throw into the gaps."

"Does everybody throw into the gaps?"

"No. Some quarterbacks throw into the seams."

"Is there any difference between throwing into a gap and throwing into a seam?"

"Somewhat, but basically a gap is a large seam. Good Lord, do you have to be so goddamned pedestrian? Like I said, the Lions are not going to go deep on this play and are very likely to send Sanders down on a curl or maybe even a fake curl ending up in a flag."

It slowly begins to register. You feel a bolt of confidence. You get reckless. "So Landry will probably try to throw into the seams to hit Sanders on the end of a curl."

"Not necessarily," he cautions, squelching your ascent into the ranks of the clairvoyants. "If you can see that coming, I would be amazed if the Viking middle linebacker can't see it. The Vikings probably will rush all-out. To beat the blitz, a quarterback must have a quick release."

"Does Landry have a quick release?"

"He has a slow release but quick reactions."

"What effect does that have?"

"It means that he's very likely to run like hell."

"So Landry is going to drop back to pass and scramble if the rush intimidates him."

"Not necessarily. The way you beat an aggressive rush like that, of course, is to use a lot of delayed plays, I mean fullback draws, screen passes, things like that. The Lions are very likely to use that in this situation."

"How do you know?"

"It's all in the frequencies. I thought everybody knew that. The Vikings have got it all down on a computer."

"So what you're saying is that the Lions will either throw to Sanders or send Landry out on a run, or run Owens up the middle on a draw or throw a little screen over Eller's head to Mel Farr."

"Yes, I think it's fair to say that."

"But you got it four different ways there. I don't see how it takes so much knowledge to say the Lions are either going to pass or run."

"Christ, you just don't see it. Even a coach when he sends in a play can't be sure the quarterback is going to call it. The defense just may come up with a different set. One of the things they may try is an Odd Man Front. This means the quarterback will try to Audible Out."

"Is Landry thinking of all of those things right now?"

"No. Right now he's thinking how he's going to save his life because here comes Page . . . "

"And there goes McCullough deep, and the one play you said couldn't happen is happening. He's throwing deep to McCullough and it's complete."

The man sits placidly, his deeper psyche unruffled by this temporary affront to his prophetic powers.

"The Vikings' defense obviously was playing Inside-Outside and somebody blew a call," he explained. "As a result the Vikings fell victim to the cardinal sin of pass defense. They allowed the Lions to Isolate a Sprinter on a Linebacker. You don't do it, you just don't do it."

The neighbor subsides into the resigned posture of the unheeded oracle.

You should understand right off there are at least three people who don't have the haziest idea what your neighbor was talking about. In order of bewilderment these are (a) Landry (b) you and (c) The Neighbor himself.

The impatient neophyte who wants to reach the same level of versatile consmanship as the neighbor has to submit to certain indignities.

It may embarrass you to have to take notes in front of your friends while announcer Johnny Sauer discloses "that punt didn't carry because it didn't turn over on its nose."

It is also awkward to have to memorize 25 times before going to bed — in order to blind your friends with some truly far-out pro talk tomorrow — "remember, you flip the safeties but flop the receivers."

The simple truth is that nobody has to sweat it that hard.

It is now possible to sound authoritative, alert, in command of the situation and even a little mysterious — in the best tradition of Coaches Tom Landry and Grant — by following a short-form training program.

It can be learned within minutes. It requires no

refresher courses, expensive subscriptions or potentially hazardous visits to the neighborhood tavern to listen to the bartender.

It is based on the sound esthetic principle that the most enduring kind of architecture is the simplest.

You do not have to complicate your version of Pro Football with the endless jabberwocky of the skull session: zig-outs, safety blitz, play-action pass and the rest of the colorman's litany.

You can rush to the forefront in neighborhood esteem by following the easy formula that will now be presented. If there is a football tyrant in the house who needs to be unhorsed, this is the deliverance.

First, you must go into action each football afternoon or evening by casually making note of the game plan. You don't have to dwell on it. The idea of some master strategy for each game, a careful blueprint, is being slowly exposed as the fraud it is. Most coaches will admit the celebrated game plan is nothing more than the list of plays on which they have worked during the week. It is called, simply and inevitably, the ready list. Most coaches, being entrenched romanticists, recognize a certain sentimental value in allowing the fan to believe the fiction of game plans. So, at least until now, they have perpetuated the harmless deception.

While your rival is going through his sorcery chants about picking on the rookie corner back or throwing sideline passes, you will unobtrusively enter the conversation and say:

"The key to this game is whether we can establish our running game."

There is nobody in the room who can argue with you.

There is nobody in the huddle who can refute you.

THERE IS NOBODY IN THE UNIVERSE who can undermine you.

Establishing the Running Game is the rock upon which this nation now stands.

It is as crucial to the ongoing security of the United States of America as the Monroe Doctrine was after the Revolutionary War. It is more than a policy; it is a creed, a faith, a condition of life.

Do not shrink from the constant repetition of this fundamental truth while the ball game is in progress. It will have an almost mesmeric effect on your slick but superficial rival.

With the score 14 to nothing and both of you beginning to stir about getting your team on the board, calmly seize control of yourself and allay all doubts about strategy by declaring:

"You've got to Establish the Running Game before anything will work."

"But the score is 14 to zip and we have not made a first down," the other will protest.

Right now you zing him with the second fundamental truth while you still have him reeling. "When you come right down to it," you say, "the name of the game is position. Now, what's the only kind of position to have in football?"

"Field position. Of course. Not only field position but Good Field Position."

"Exactly. You've got to establish the running game to get good field position."

He knows without dispute that you have just spelled out one of the unshatterable maxims of life as we know it in the 20th Century.

How lame and inconsequential his zig-outs and banana patterns sound alongside that.

With the score now having mounted to 24-0 against your athletes, it is time to introduce new material into your analysis, "putting in more of the offense," in the language of the coaches.

"What do you think they're going to do now?" the other will ask.

"Well, even though they are behind 24-0 they're not going to open up the defense consistently until they Run At the Defense's Strength.'

"Which is just another way of saying . . .

"We've Got to Take it To Them. To win this game we've got to establish the ground game by taking it to them and running at their strength."

"But haven't we been doing that for three quarters?"

"Yes. But the quarterback knows that You've Got to Be Patient."

That will do it. No matter what happens the rest of the game, you have displayed your sure-fingered grasp of the crucial elements of the game. You have profiled its very character.

And so does it matter that your team finally expires, although grudgingly, 49-0?

The team has kept the faith.

You have kept the faith.

That short-form again, and remember the sequence, because it is important. This is all you need say during a ballgame to silence all the others as skin-deep charlatans:

1. Establish the Running Game.
2. Get Good Field Position.
3. Run at Their Strength.
4. Take It To Them.
   (These latter two, under certain conditions are interchangeable.)
5. You Have To Be Patient.

They can be used singly or in combination, at practically any stage of the ball game. They are fool-proof and can be spoken either in the form of a prophecy, critique or off-hand observation.

I don't think any clinching show of expertise is needed, but if it is, whenever there is a lull or tension in the room, stand up and shout.

"DE-fense, DE-fense, DE-fense."

You are now accepted as a bona fide aficionado beyond the last threads of doubt. You don't even have to kick the extra point.

The Night the Announcers Fired Cuozzo

With the possible exception of the Fuller Brush salesman, no institution in America has been subjected to as much surface contempt and private awe as the TV football analyst.

His craft has reached that rare literary estate attained only by the biographer Boswell. The reading crowd now talks more about Boswell than about Johnson, the one he biographed. The television crowd today, especially after a game decided by five field goals and a safety, talks more about the analyst than the analyzees.

More public rage, devotion and bafflement was directed last fall, for example, at Howard Cosell than at the Detroit Lions in their urgent futilities against the Minnesota Vikings.

This is no empty generalization. There are two authorities who support it: (1) Howard Cosell and (2) Howard Cosell's press attache, frequently identified as Howard Cosell.

Two clashing views of Howard as telecaster and unquenchable authority have rent the nation and threatened international upheavals the past couple of years.

The first represents Howard as obnoxious and a

Haven at the lake

Haven Books

Diane Dorr-Ruzin

Crosslake, MN 56442

14043 Swann Drive PO Box 655

haven@crosslake.net

New and Used books

218.692.5010

pain in the tail only in a superficial way; that beneath this calculated, show business braggadocio there is a man of thoughtfulness, candor, burning social consciousness, savoir faire, good hearted humor and kindness to lost squirrels. Among those advancing this viewpoint is Howard Cosell.

The other looks on Howard as a needless burden on a people already afflicted with high taxes, crab grass and bad air.

Few people in public life have been so relentlessly psycho-analyzed. According to Howard's intimates the last one accorded such treatment, at least with comparable exposure over a long period of time, was the Emperor Nero.

Actually, there is no need to take sides. Those partial to Monday night football should understand that Howard's modest, first assessment of his role a couple of years ago was absolutely correct. He is no analyst. Occasionally he puts on the robes of reporter. In his calmer moments Howard might be the first to acknowledge that his self-constructed image as a fearless journalist is somewhat overdrawn. He is totally fearless, for example, when he describes a turkey football game as "no artistic gem, this." But he is only mildly fearless when approaching the sacred elephants of, say, Carol Rosenbloom, the owner of the Los Angeles Rams.

To be enjoyed, Howard has to be looked on as a super, self-propelled provocateur and gadfly, filled with formidable trivia. He gives the impression of a man frustrated by a twist of destiny that has deprived him of a suitable forum for his art. As a result he has to make do, acting as straight-man for the barnyard bon mots of Don Meredith, tolerating Frank Gifford and reminding us histor-ically that this is the selfsame Gilliam who ran back the opening kickoff 98 yards in the first game the New Orleans Saints ever inflicted on the public. Did you realize that Dandy?

"No, Howard," Dandy replies gravely, "I didn't realize that until this very moment when you said it. But if you said it, Howard, I guess it must be true."

Most television watchers go through predictable phases in their exposure to this kind of theater, as the people did when first struck by burlesque. In the first few months it moves smoothly from mild annoyance to smouldering outrage — attitudes which undoubtedly accosted Gifford himself. But the really durable person will always find a way to adapt. If you live in a floodplain long enough you are eventually going to build a boat. Most football watchers now live amiably with Cosell and Mere-dith. Among them, apparently, is Frank Gifford.

I put myself in this number. Cosell invariably suggests to me a man who has fought the good fight with the demands of humility and restraint, and abandoned it as an unequal struggle. Viewed from this perspective he is highly entertaining, much more so, at least, than the fair catches and busted field goals that now represent a sizeable part of the typical National Football League game action.

Howard is unbelievable only when he pretends it is his wisdom and candor which makes him unique on football television, rather than his carefully rehearsed insufferability.

He will profess disdain, privately and publicly, for announcers who dip into the coaches' vocabulary for their analytic musings. We talked about it for awhile last year. "You hear announcers telling the viewers about Al Davis and the hash mark zone," he groaned. "THE HASH MARK ZONE." If I used that, two million people would turn on the Carol Burnette Show right now. You'll hear some announcer say, 'hey, Pat, you see what Francis is doing. He's picking on the rookie cornerback. He wants to isolate Tucker on the rookie.' That kind of stuff. It's stagnation. What the hell does the fan care about the hash mark zone or the slip screen. He wants to know how the fullback happened to get arrested at 2 in the morning in Weehawken."

It is such intrepid reportage, Howard confessed, "that draws more and more women to listen to and watch Howard Cosell," certainly more than would be attracted by the simple virility of Frank Gifford. In this he is unquestionably correct, since Gifford is further handicapped by such impediments as giving the score and the down and distance.

Is Howard Cosell, then, the new Valentino of American entertainment?

Howard lowered his eyes and smiled becomingly.

There are some qualities, he seemed to be saying, that a man simply cannot acknowledge publicly.

"But I'll say this. Everybody was looking for Cosell to bomb. I was ready for it, the Dick Youngs and the super-critics. You can't realize the ferocity of it. But they came around and were saying happying things about me in the end. I mean Jim Murray, Mel Durslag, all the ones who count.

"You know, of course, that at a very early period Meredith was ready to throw in the jock. Somebody had ripped him up and down for one of his early performances. He said, 'Howie, I can't do what they want. Hell, I know the X's and the O's, but I can't be what they want me to be.' And I took him aside and I said, 'Dandy, you're crazy. You're gonna be a folk hero with all that back country happy stuff. I'm the guy who will wear the black hat. We'll be a smash.'

"Which, I need hardly add, we were.

"The ratings, good at the beginning, soared. What made it all the more impressive was some of the dog games they gave us in that first year."

The implication here is that someday the National Football League is just going to have to get around to conceding the NFL's imperishable debt to Howard Cosell for sustaining it through one of its darkest hours — the period when it commanded only six consecutive hours of Sunday television time.

The key, not only to coping with but enjoying Gifford, Meredith and Cosell (you can refer to them as the GMC of the Monday night jock strap trade) is to understand the juicy irony of their distribution of work. Gifford, an ex-footballer, does what they used to train fallen-away disc jockeys to do, which is the play-by-play. Meredith, another ex-footballer, does what the networks trained re-formed jugglers to do, which is to provide the comedy. Both have quick minds and are as authoritative on football as anybody on earth.

Howard is unshaken by this powerhouse of football wisdom. He allows Meredith to explain what went wrong with the little square-out. And then he smoothly volunteers to tell us what the game is all about, as explained to him at lunch that noon by Tom Landry.

Although Cosell is still abrasive to millions, and Meredith sometimes is indistinguishable from Pat Buttram, the majority of the Monday night oglers usually find themselves stimulated. Beyond this, with the mounting epidemic of 6-3 football games in the NFL, the pie-throwing is sometimes indispensable.

Once every three or four weeks, however, when the moon is right and either Cosell or Meredith has had the wrong fare for lunch, GMC will have the sound of the old Marx Brothers trying to describe the Klondike gold rush.

Such a magical hour occurred Sept. 25, 1971, at Tiger Stadium in Detroit when the Detroit Lions met the Minnesota Vikings in the opening game of the season.

The Lions came on like the Mafia's revenge for Leif Erickson. On the first four sequences the Vikings either fumbled or got scored on. After eight minutes the Lions outpossessed them, in the language of the game statistician, 22 times to 1. At a very early point Meredith and Cosell, alternating with the microphone in the style of Blanchard and Davis, began preparing their teeming audience for the news that Norman Snead would soon replace Gary Cuozzo at quarterback for the Vikings.

Cosell has since denied any complicity in this public service, laying all the credit to Meredith, but he draws no comfort from the replayed tapes.

As the quarter wears on and the Vikings continue to get outpossessed, Meredith and Cosell express growing amazement that Bud Grant has not yet ratified the ABC decision to go with Snead. The wish, ultimately, sires the deed. Sometime near the end of the first quarter Frank Gifford puts an end to the suspense. He appeases the clamoring couple and puts Norm Snead in the game in place of the unfortunate Cuozzo.

One play later Cuozzo is back in the game, which may surprise the teeming millions but does not faze Bud Grant at all. Bud is the only one in the country, evidently, who is unaware that Bud Grant has changed quarterbacks. The reason for this innocence is clear enough. Cuozzo never left the field. Meredith had the wrong guy.

Don considerately accepts the horns for mistaking Snead's No. 16 for Cuozzo's No. 15. Meanwhile, down on the field, Gary seems oblivious of his imminent exile and is throwing completions with snappy abandon. Some of the audience comprehends this. Certainly Lem Barney of the Lions does, since Lem is being methodically shredded by Cuozzo and Bobby Grim.

The news so far has managed to elude Meredith and Cosell, who have been distracted trying to get Snead into the game.

To help relieve the identity gap, the camera now fixes inquisitively on Bud Grant at the Viking bench. His team is bumbling and the hostile crowd is catcalling but Bud stands there, immovable and inscrutable, the face of forever. He seems part of the geography, a piece of the continent.

Don Meredith, although Texan, is broad-minded enough to forgive the North for winning the Civil War. But he has never forgiven the North for Green Bay, cold weather and other foreign qualities. Or it might be that Bud's unearthly ability to endure long periods of inept play by his warriors without rushing into the nearest cement mixer reminds him of his own old coach, Tom Landry. Whatever the provocation, Don regards Bud's untwitching features on the screen and bursts into melody:

"You are my sunshine, my only sunshine."

Howard now dons the robes of gallantry and reminds Meredith that Bud Grant is a good and excellent man who doesn't panic.

The Lions' Tommy Vaughn intercepts a pass.

Howard starts moving toward his closet for another robe.

"Maybe," he says, "Bud Grant SHOULD start to panic and move to a guy named Snead."

With this Gifford begins to quiver once more. They are going to try to run Snead in on him again. When Jones dives into the Lions' line Gifford declares, "and that's the end of the first half."

This announcement unsettles several parties, including the audience, the producer and the time-keeper, whose watch shows 10 minutes still remaining in the first half.

Frank recovers splendidly. He explains somebody slipped him the wrong card. Certainly no fair-minded viewer is going to quibble with this excuse. Still, he has to wonder what would have happened in televisionland if somebody slipped Frank a card declaring the Martians had just landed at Ottumwa, Iowa, and were moving on Dubuque.

It begins to look like Black Rock for the Vikings. GMC start to recapitulate the ruin wrought on the Vikings through the first 20 minutes, and as George Wallace used to tell his listeners, "when the co-ordinators begin recapitulatin' on you, people, it's bad, real bad."

Howard flatly pictures the Vikings as lying help-less before the fury of the Lions. Don averts his eyes from the devastation momentarily to chide Carl Eller, who has just flattened Greg Landry, the Lions' quarterback. "Carl," he says, "be nice to those boys (the quarterbacks). They're gentle.

They got mothers just like you."

The Lions' lead jumps to 13-0 in the second period. Don clearly does not want to be rude and come right out and repudiate Bud as a hopeless Horatio defending lost causes. But neither can he abdicate his responsibility as the voice of football's conscience.

"Again I want to remind you of the possibility that we might see Norm Snead in the second half."

"I think you're right," Howard agrees. "I think they're going to work on Dick LeBeau, the veteran cornerback, whom some feel may have lost a step or so."

For the moment you will certainly want to dismiss the ignoble thought that this is the selfsame Howard who roasted a nameless colleague for saying, 'hey Pat, you see what Francis is doing. He's picking on the rookie cornerback. He wants to isolate Tucker on the rookie.'

But it is left to Don, a tolerant man despite his preference for manure-kicking ballplayers, to make the sudden discovery that Gary Cuozzo is playing a great football game.

"He's hitting 9 for 13," Don advises all of the fans from coast to coast who have been breathlessly awaiting the arrival of Norm Snead. "That's 69 per cent, and that ain't bad."

His confidence surely restored by Don's assurances, Cuozzo goes to the sideline to confer with Grant with the ball inside the Lions' 10.

"What's going on in this conference between the

coach and quarterback?" Howard says, deftly setting up a lob.

"He's saying 'son, it's up to you.'"

But Dandy adds this double-edged prophecy:

"With second down and 13 seconds to go and no more time outs, you can only assume Bud Grant's saying we've got to go for the touchdown. Maybe they can get off two passes at the most. I think you'll see him throw a pattern that's relatively safe. What that is I don't know, because they can all be picked off."

There's just no way getting around it, they can, and that's a fact.

Realizing this, Bud tells Gary to pick a pattern that's relatively safe, although he adds that they can all be picked off, Gary, and please remember that.

By unanimous vote Gary picks a pattern that is relatively safe. That accomplished, the pass falls routinely incomplete and Fred Cox kicks a field goal to reduce the score to 13-3. The Vikings now lie a little less helpless before the fury of the Lions.

By way of proof, Cuozzo in the fourth minute of the third period throws a 45-yard touchdown pass to Grim, upon whom Barney never lays a glove.

The least surprised by this development, he tells us, is Howard Cosell himself.

"I told you, gentlemen, they're going more and more at Barney these days," he confirms. "They started doing it last year when Dick Gordon (of the Bears) showed them it could be done."

You can now fully appreciate the symmetrical beauty of Howard's forecasts. He has already prepared us for the probability of the Vikings working on Dick LeBeau, the venerable right cornerback who was diagnosed as practically lame.

In his updated analysis Cosell reveals that the Vikings will be going after the left cornerback, Barney, in addition to going after LeBeau. This puts both the fan and Howard in that never-never land of the football mystic, wherein no matter which cornerback Cuozzo goes after, we're covered. The logic in this is indestructible. There are only two Lions' cornerbacks on the field.

Chalk one up for native shrewdness.

Cuozzo is happily throwing pass completions. His average now climbs to 71 per cent. The Vikings lead 16-13. Howard instinctively finds the crux of the drama. He outlines it in those clean, sweeping strokes of the Moving Finger, the chronicler of the life's grand designs.

"What a turn of events. At the start of the game Gary Cuozzo in desperate trouble. The three of us talking about the possibility of Snead showing up soon. Now if the Vikings win, Cuozzo has engineered the victory. That's what I mean about Bud Grant, a poised coach. Don't underestimate this man, Don."

This is the kind of consummate art you want to be watching for on Monday nights. It will maximize your viewing pleasure. In one stunning declarative paragraph Howard has:

Tied the can to Cuozzo's tail for the Vikings' early

offensive futility, although it was the fumbling Viking backs who were the bunglers, not the quarterback.

Implicated the defenseless and innocent Gifford in the Cosell-Meredith decision to cashier Cuozzo.

Dumped the whole bundle on Meredith's head by slyly suggesting that Howard's hip-shooting buddy should have listened to Howard all along in order to avoid embarrassing the others.

"He makes changes slowly, Don," Howard continues sublimely, filling the air with a merry shower of soap flakes that obliterates all traces of Howard's own advice to Grant to get rid of Cuozzo.

"Don't underestimate this man, Don," he says. "He knows what he's doing."

Meredith barely manages to escape the blizzard.

"I wouldn't underrate him for anything. I'm more impressed with Cuozzo right now than I am with Bud Grant."

Together the three of them march forward purposefully, toward the inevitable climax when Erroll Mann blows a 32 yard field goal that would have tied the game in the final minute for Detroit.

It was a narrow escape. What if Mann had made it? I don't believe the TV audience was ready for what would have been the curtain speech of the evening:

"Never underestimate Joe Schmidt and the Lions, Don. It may take them a while, but they get things done."

Mark X for Your Favorite Genius

The most carefully suppressed document in American advertising is a scouting report on the TV announcers. It was compiled by a blue ribbon commission at the request of one of the network maharajahs.

The document's existence is not generally known by the football crowd. Certain portions of it evidently have been leaked because I am now able to reveal intimate evaluations intended only for highly placed executives in the industry.

Remember, these are from the raw files. They are intended primarily as a guide in your selection process at the TV dial and to help you in rating the psychic power of the various wise men.

Each viewer is entitled to make his own margin notes. These in turn might well turn up in some future commission report in which the viewers are rated by the television announcers.

JACK WHITTAKER — Workmanlike and usually photogenic although he tends to be confused sometimes by the analysis expert, Tom Brookshier. This is a fate that could overtake anyone. Jack needs to learn how to audible off quickly when Brookshier starts talking about his old days with the Philadelphia Eagles and Van Brocklin.

CURT GOWDY — Still one of the most listenable play-by-play announcers in the pros although he has not quite recovered from his immoderate fondness for the Kansas City Chiefs and the American Football League. He performed a valuable service for a time by keeping Kyle Rote, the color announcer, awake.

RAY SCOTT — Reliable, dramatic and full of orotund sounds and syllables. These are arresting enough to make a simple station break sound like the potential turning point of the game. Ray should someday be assigned to do an all-network game with Howard Cosell, for which tickets would be sold not to the game but the broadcasting booth. Stung by Cosell's "hey, Pat" (presumably for Summerall) innuendoes, Scott has come to regard Cosell as a hoax, a blight on the trade, a kilocycled headhunter and generally a soupstain on the industry's shirt-front.

FRANK GIFFORD — Frank must now serve penance for years of untroubled success as a player by being forced to mediate the Don and Howie Show on Monday nights. This he does uniformly well and with only an occasional groan of defiance. Like other converted jocks, Frank will sometimes forget that not all television watchers were born in a whirlpool bath. At these times he might tap you lightly with this, from a Lions' game last year:

"The fans might be wondering how you can send both of your backs out without the blitz killing your quarterback. But both of those backs are stepping up, and when they see there is no blitz, they flare out into the flat on the checkoff."

The question is, were you really wondering that strenuously, fans?

AL DEROGATIS — This is the Einstein of the color analysts, the only one who by constant repetition has taught the grandmothers of America the difference between a fold block and an influence trap. It is not unusual to hear Al describe how the Dolphins secondary was playing Inside-Outside against the Jets' receivers and how the Jets countered by going Topside instead of Underside. He is one of the few network announcers who goes to work with a chalk and blackboard instead of an atomizer. Al is sound and dependable, although devotedly humorless. Al's conception of a one-liner is to remind the audience that it is the third quarter and the Patriots still haven't run a slip screen to the short side of the field.

PAT SUMMERALL — Probably the best of the two-way color announcers on network television, meaning he usually makes sense when he talks and he does an outstanding job of keeping quiet when unneeded. It may have escaped the attention of all but the most discerning analyst-monitors, however, that Pat has developed a crafty technique of predicting what will happen on the next play — without actually predicting it. There was the interlude in a 49er-Dallas game on which Pat teamed with Ray Scott:

SUMMERALL: "I can't help but remember two weeks ago when the 49ers were in a similar situation against Oakland. John Brodie had third and one. And he faked to Ken Willard in a dive into the left side of his line, and hit Witcher with a touchdown pass . . ."

The ball is snapped and the lines collide.

SCOTT: "Willard is nailed for a loss back at the 49-yard line of San Francisco."

It left the viewer in an interesting dilemma: On this play, was Summerall a lousy prophet, or a good quarterback?

JOHNNY SAUER — Talkative but fascinating. Johnny is a former college and pro coach and scout who delivers a color commentary as though he were lecturing a class of high school coaches. He was credited with delivering both the season's sapphire and its lead brick within a span of five minutes during a game at San Diego.

John was describing the technique whereby a tackler deliberately peels the ball from an onrushing back. He declared:

"I think we should point out right now that the best stripper in professional football is Alan Page of the Minnesota Vikings."

Page almost demanded equal time to respond the next day after hearing about John's remarkable characterization.

And yet John reached Valhalla a few minutes later when Norman Snead entered the game in place of Gary Cuozzo with the Vikings trailing by three points.

"The thing you have to worry about here," he said, "is Snead's tendency to throw the ball into the middle. He's a good passer, but that's where you're most likely to get yourself intercepted."

On the very next play, Norman Snead threw the ball up the middle.

And San Diego intercepted.

HOWARD COSELL — In the judgment of some, including Howard, he is matched only by Richard Nixon in influence and visibility. For all his attainments, his closest associates contend, Howard has yet to match on TV the heights he achieved as a color man in the filming of the movie "Bananas" starring Woody Allen as Fielding Mellish. In this sequence, Howard did the color on the consummation of Mellish's marriage.

"This is tremendous, just tremendous, fans . . . the first live coverage of an actual honeymoon night . . .

"Here comes the bride . . . she's entering the room first and she's got many fans here . . . she looks in good condition. And here comes Mellish. He's wearing a green corduroy suit . . . jogging and bobbing down the aisle with his trainers . . . He looks in unbelievable physical condition for a honeymoon . . . I know he's trained for it very hard . . . he really wants this one . . . he's been going around telling everyone he's the greatest . . . "

I didn't have the heart to stick around to find out whether Mellish made the conversion.

DON MEREDITH — Likeable and authoritative, the fraternity man's Dizzy Dean. Don has acquired a cozy professionalism since his unforgetable night two years ago when he walked out of the door, heartsick and betrayed, at the sight of his Cowboys being creamed by the St. Louis Cardinals:

"I don't see anybody hitting out there and I don't see much tackling either. They were more than confused on the last play. They were lost.

"Howard, I had so many funny stories to tell but I'm so upset I can't tell funny stories while this stuff's goin' on out there. There's another that Werle almost intercepted. That one was underthrown. Oh, me."

COSELL: "It's almost incredible that a team with Hayes, Lilly, Hill, Renfro, Pettis Norman and others could look so futile."

MEREDITH: "Howard, you missed the offensive line, which is also a great bunch of athletes. Howard, you'll never know what trouble is until you're 17 points behind in the Cotton Bowl."

And Donald never knew what trouble is until

he got the mail from St. Louis on Tuesday.

TOM BROOKSHIER — One of the few men in the football TV craft who is a self-designated comedian. With these credentials Tom fills his commentary with such expressions as "hog bladder" for football and "ah, for the life of a quarterback, it looks like convertibles and bright lights but it's a miserable way to spend Sunday afternoon."

With such ripostes, and his tribalistic half dozen allusions each game to "the old Dutchman," Brookshier quickly qualified for the roster of the CBS Super Bowl team.

And it fell to Tom Brookshier to do the interview of the decade, the post-game dialogue in which the disenchanted Dallas halfback, Duane Thomas, broke three months of silence and agreed to submit to an interview.

They stood there on the retreaded apple boxes CBS uses for the clubhouse interviews. There was Brookshier, there was Thomas' and Duane's governess, Jim Brown. The audience was enormous. Dallas had just won the Super Bowl, and here was the Big Exclusive, the moment when Duane Thomas tells all to his worshipping but puzzled fans.

Tom gulped, just perceptibly, and launched an avalanche of words. This was calculated to cover up any hint of dead air and to goad Thomas into lyrical flights of rhetoric.

"Duane," he began, "how are you?"

47

DUANE: "All right."

BROOKSHIER: "My name's Tom Brookshier. Nice to talk to you, and behind you is a fellow who used to run over me for a living, the great Jimmy Brown. How are you, Jimmy?"

BROWN: "Fine, Tom, how are you?"

BROOKSHIER: "Duane, you do things with speed, but you never hurry. A lot like the great Jim Brown. You never hurry into a hole. You take your time, make a spin, you still outrun people. Are you that fast, Duane? Are you that quick? Would you say?"

Duane examines the question cautiously. With millions of viewers hanging on his answer and Brookshier gushing gallons of sweat, Thomas replies:

"Evidently."

Having scored this coup, Brookshier storms on with the interview.

"One time John Niland was leading a sweep, Duane, and he didn't get a good block. He didn't get good position. And you simply stepped around him and turned up the sidelines."

In the lexicon of the trade, this is generally known as a CUE!

It was so much a cue that Brookshier wanted to scream, "that's a cue, Duane. Duane, I mean would you consider that a cue, Duane?"

Cue or not, it was profoundly clear Duane was not about to deliver two great orations on the same show.

BROOKSHIER: "Jimmy, maybe you can answer it for us. Jimmy, doesn't he have a little more speed than it appears?"

BROWN: "Actually, Duane is one of the most gifted runners in football today. He's big and he has fantastic moves. I think he's as smart as any football player playing today. With that combination, he's fantastic. He has great intellect."

BROOKSHIER (fervently pursuing at least Word 2 from the star of the interview on this coast-to-coast production): "Duane, people don't know this. People don't know, but I know this. And I know this is a sort of a tight situation . . . "

BROWN: "What, are you nervous Tom?"

BROOKSHIER: "I'm nervous. Duane. People tell me you run further with the ball in practice than anyone. You must like the game. YOU MUST LIKE THE GAME OF FOOTBALL!"

DUANE (alerted by what might vaguely strike him as a controversial question): "Yeah, I do. That's why I went out for pro ball. You know, that's why I am a football player. So that's why I produce."

BROOKSHIER: "I'll tell you, you're some kind of a football player. Pat Summerall commented during the game that you might be bigger than 205. Is 205 accurate? Or do you go about 215?"

DUANE (after giving the impression of agonizing over this two-pronged challenge): "It all depends on what I need."

BROOKSHIER: "You mean you wear different weights for different teams?"

DUANE: "Sure."

On this definitive chord, the interview ends.

The moral is: Be gentle with television analysts. They have mothers just like you.

The Reformation of Annie

Sociologists say the most fearsome sight on the American scene today is the educated woman who once scorned football but is now totally evangelized.

Nobody has as much passion as the freshly reformed. You have the millionaire's daughter who learned the joys of the proletarian life, the converted spinster who has suddenly and exuberantly acquired a stable of exhausted swains. And now the newly-inflamed football madames.

The mania has afflicted women more than is generally realized.

Nobody denies there are formidable numbers of American housewives wounded or appalled by the conduct of their football freak husbands. But the TV surveyors will tell you nearly as many women watch the game as men, not as rowdily or as ferociously perhaps, but with at least some kind of fugitive curiosity.

The experts don't agree on the reasons for it. There is a type of woman that will be lifted into an aboriginal frenzy by the sight of a professional wrestler, a weight lifter or a high diver. None of these wears much more than is required by local ordinance or the demands of self-preservation.

For dedicated body watchers the attraction is clear enough. But what of football players in full armor? All have to be outfitted by the quartermaster, the trainer, the equipment manager, the doctor and the metalsmith. By this time they exude the same kind of sex magnetism as King Tut the Mummy.

And so you will get learned theories on why so many women are drawn to pro football. These range from their celebrated yen for secrets (the huddle) to the unspoken urge to experience something more disorganized than their own household (most screen passes on third and long).

I say horsefeathers to most of these.

By and large, American women watch pro football in self-defense. They may have a glancing interest in it. But almost all of them who watch it with their husbands do it from the mortal dread of being made social and conversational outcasts for the weekend.

To those women who do look at football with the same apoplectic grimness as the marathon squatters among the men, let me say this: Neither blush for it nor let yourselves be misused for it. Carry your beanies proudly! Stand erect in your stadium boots!

I say this in sadness for the disgraceful fate that overtook a college language instructor from St. Cloud, Minn., Annie Fleischer, a living, frothing football maniac.

Mrs. Fleischer has given a deposition. She says she would have preferred a more dignified role on

Sunday afternoons. But the truth was she became a kind of talisman, a lucky pendant, for her husband's football klatsch.

At a very early date in her conversion to pro football it was discovered that whenever Mrs. Fleischer went to the bathroom, inexplicably good things happened to her favorite team, the Minnesota Vikings.

I hesitate to tell you what National Football League record Mrs. Fleischer holds in terms of consecutive number of successful tries.

As a signal lesson in what women football fans should avoid at all costs, Mrs. Fleischer consents to share her self-critique.

"I actively loathed football until four seasons ago," she says. "My idea of a big date in college was not going to the Saturday game. A few times I weakened. The last time I remember was a game between Illinois and Indiana. I froze to the seat. I literally had to be pried off.

"Later, at the health center, where I was treated for a variety of diseases including frozen behind, I had the extreme good luck to be visited upon by an injured football player.

"I have relegated his name to the oblivion it deserves. But he had a crew cut, smoked black cigars, and had an inexhaustible supply of BS. He cured me of ever wanting to make the football effort again, and I put football and football players well down on my list. A little bit above, say, hypocrisy and fratricide. But not much.

"I had a few quiet and pleasant years . . .

"And then I got married. To a football fan. I didn't expect him to be a football fan. He wears a vest, carries a black umbrella and his pipe tobacco is a special blend out of New York at seven dollars a pound. Which just goes to show that when you meet somebody and get married, you never know what skeletons you're going to find. At any rate, he's of Hungarian temperament and runs his house. We wound up going to the Twin Cities every weekend that the game wasn't blacked out, and we would watch TV with friends who fall into the fan category.

"At that time we were bedded down on an extremely unfriendly couch that we later came to call The Rack. The Rack was in the living room with the TV. So I had to do my best at sawing off a few extra Z's with three screaming idiots on all sides.

"This continued until one afternoon when I happened to have an eye open. Almost unavoidably I directed it to the TV. I watched a play that must have been some Joe Kapp maim-the-linebacker special. I don't think it was planned. But it was memorable. And it, well, it shook out all my apathy and turned me into a fan. It would be comforting to say that being a fan at our place involved nothing more than keeping the fridge filled with beer and the table piled with pretzels and cheese. But getting hooked at my age is like getting the mumps when you're over 20. You don't get off easily.

"The season was into November when this friend

remarked, 'have you noticed that when Annie goes to the bathroom the play works?'

"Such a wild proposition, of course, has to be tested. It was. A true neophyte, I did what I was told. And every time I heard Oh-My-God-He's-Going-to-Throw-It I knew I was about to be sent back to the WC. (I remember the 1968 season as white tile and orange and rust bathmat.)

"This was all very well and good, but it began to pale after I realized that while everybody else was screaming about post patterns and curls and watching the game, I wasn't doing anything but helping the Scott shareholders.

"This struck me as rather unfair and I said so.

"Had I been talking to normal people, mine would have been a reasonable attitude. But there was nothing normal about that mob. They had been fans from the beginning. It was like a Russian politician being able to trace his credentials back to the revolution. But I stood my ground and sometimes I went and sometimes I didn't and sometimes I didn't even watch. That was the only football season that I truly enjoyed myself.

"In 1969 I learned how to scream.

"The Go-To-The-Bathroom-Annie is such a standard in this house that the only people who take note of it now are non-footballers. Friends of ours yelled it at Metropolitan Stadium. I will never publicly confess what I yelled back.

"To this day I refuse to see another game at the stadium. Don't get me wrong. The excitement is

great. The only problem is with the logistics. Our seats were 200 yards from the nearest facility.

"So here I am, after three and a half years of it, a true hardcore about football. I knew I'd crossed the line between fan and idiot when I found myself in the middle of a tirade at a downtown liquor store. Some heretic made the statement that he was going to give up the Vikings because they couldn't win the championship. Never before or since have I been able to rattle off football statistics the way I did that afternoon. I walked out on him while he still had one hand in the air and his mouth open. With a clock in his stomach he would have made a fine wedding present for somebody with a large living room. I came home and told my husband what I'd done. He put his hands over his face and simply said, 'Oh, my God.'

"It's all very simple. Around here you can tell jokes about the Pope, say that the house is ugly, that my mother has a strange sense of humor and that somebody else makes a better roast suckling pig than I do. But everybody under this roof is deadly serious about one thing: You always take the ball on the kickoff. You never take the wind.

"My addiction produces a few gasps from friends and a sign of sympathy now and then. A priest once told me: 'you're not real. How can anybody who goes to the Prado, reads Spanish literature and teaches poetry wear a hat and shirt like that and take it SERIOUSLY.'

"I think my husband is convinced he has created some kind of monster.

"When they first asked him about what kind of football cluck he was living with he said, 'oh, I guess it hasn't changed so much around here.' A couple of weeks later he confronted me in the kitchen and said, 'I'll hang up your damn football poster, but you'll have to give up the towel rack if I do.'

"Two weeks later I heard him bitching to a friend on the phone, 'I LIVE IN THE ONLY HOUSE IN THE WORLD THAT DOESN'T HAVE A TOWEL RACK IN THE KITCHEN.'

"And the last week of the season he stood up in the middle of dinner and said, 'I can't even get a beer out of the refrigerator without looking at a picture of Bill Brown. You can put him up all over the kitchen and Osborn in the study and Eller in the dining room — but keep them the hell out of the bedroom, will you?'

"Well, that almost did it. For consolation I visited with my father. We got to talking about Kansas City and that replay of the Super Bowl where the Chiefs' coach, Hank Stram, was wired and said some snippy things about the Vikings. The more I thought about Stram the madder I got. I found my father staring at me sort of stunned. 'Where,' he asked, 'did you learn to talk like that? Don't let your mother hear you.'"

But she no longer plods to the bathroom

on command.

What further evidence is needed that Annie has made it to the big leagues?

Save the Mayonnaise for 4th Down

The saga of Annie really belongs in the Cro-Magnon era of the football viewing culture.

No self-respecting woman is going to submit to exile in the comfort station today simply because the old man is trying to promote a first down. I grant there may be remnants of it, especially if you're looking at a field goal from a bad angle.

But as long as America is charging brazenly into this awakening golden age of emancipation, isn't it about time we outgrew the beer and cheese devotionals?

I have known strong, durable men who withstood four straight blown field goals by the home team in the last five minutes only to collapse of aggravated gastritis from four bags of Chee-tos.

My cousin from the republic of Switzerland was a house guest last fall. He is not a chef but does have the typical European's admiration for unhurried dining as an exercise in civilization, the one activity that separates man from the lower primates.

We watched the Packers and Bears. It was a game in which I had a clinical interest but no supercharged passion. Because of this I did not put in the usual fresh supplies from the neighborhood commissary, there being no particular need to fortify myself with high-yield, day-of-battle groceries.

Nonetheless, my European cousin was an interested spectator. After two quarters of nondescript football, he re-focused from the screen to me.

"You must be doing this in jest," he declared. "This cannot be your normal Sunday dining programme."

"That's correct," I said, unintimidated. "On normal Sundays I lean more toward the dips and spreads. It is a simple maneuver to cover a Melba toast wafer with french-onion spread without losing eyeball contact with the line-blocking. If you go to the salads, on the other hand, you have to make visual adjustments as you go along and you miss a good deal of the action."

"But does everybody in America stuff himself in this manner during a football game?" he pressed.

"Gout sufferers and convalescents on a salt-free diet have trouble staying with the pack," I replied. "Otherwise, yes, it's rather universal."

My cousin was reared in the traditions of social graces. He tried to share in the mound of squirrel food before him, but dropped off shortly after the start of the third quarter, badly routed and dimly stupefied.

I suppose we shouldn't be too harsh with his show of timidity. When you come to think of it, we ARE performing some kind of gastronomic barbarism on Sunday afternoons.

By instinct I am not a heavy eater. Six years ago I chose the road to redemption and trimmed 55 pounds in five months of wild-eyed dieting. Even before that I never ate much, but I did eat badly. My reformation is now total — with the single weekly exception of Sunday afternoon, when frankly, deliberately and without any special remorse I gorge myself abominably.

I practice the usual deceptions. Because Cheez-it crackers are small and look uniformly innocent, I will go through at least two boxes on a Sunday afternoon. These I augment with taco-flavored Doritos (usually in the first half of double-headers to permit settling of the body juices later on) and a bland, alien little low-calorie biscuit called "dietetic kuchels," a product of the Stella D'Oro ovens.

I'll tell you about dietetic kuchels. There was a time when they were in their prime and nothing could touch them on the snacking tray for versatility and simple class. That was in the cyclamates era. The federal government in 1970 decided to ban cyclamates. In its impact on calorie-watching TV football fans, this had the same effect as the NFL's decision to ban the play where a ball-carrier could get up and run after being tackled unless he had been physically interred.

What it did was take some of the gusto out of the game. Kuchels are still active and remain on my reserve tray at eight calories per biscuit, but in a way it's like seeing a revered veteran trying to make a comeback. You somehow feel a catch in your throat.

For greens and eye-strengthening food value I stick mostly with serrated raw carrots, radishes, dill pickles, lettuce-salad (pre-game, because it does become a distraction after that) and on rare occasions, celery stalks. These are extremely noisy, though, and at times drown out some of the more subdued color announcers, such as Kyle Rote and Willie Davis.

My staples are Melba toast wafers (the 1" by 2-1/2" rectangles, with a caloric rating of 16), covered lightly with hickory-smoked cheese from the aerosol can. Sometimes I go to cheddar if the action dawdles. For a change of pace I switch to matzo crackers, the diet-thin version, sold at most Jewish delicatessens but not always recommended, I understand, for kosher use. These I have found excellent as staging platforms for the Underwood's potted deviled ham that has become my standard fare in the fourth quarter of close games.

I gave up beer-drinking six years ago as part of my slimming program. Except for one evening in Munich where I was threatened with subpoenas and deportation for trying to introduce this madness to Germany, I have avoided it since. I have nothing against beer. It comes down to a matter of mathematics. I still count calories, using a special mini-abacus that fits into one of the card compartments of my wallet. Most of the diet manuals rate beer at 150 calories, — 135, I suppose, if you drink Coors. The plain truth is that I prefer to take my calories, even on Sunday, in solid form. I fully appreciate that a bag of taco-flavored Doritos may pack double or triple the calorie content of a bottle of beer. Call it an aberration. Like the playing rosters of the pro football teams, the ranks of the football watchers are smattered with free-falling eccentrics usually characterized as flakes.

Am I a Sunday afternoon flake?

My wife is convinced of it.

"The only thing that makes sense about your schlocky Sunday smorgasbord is what you drink," she tells me. "I think your normal consumption of two six-packs of Fresca can be defended. I certainly know it can't be surpassed."

In every football televiewer's offense there should be at least one department in which he excels, one phase about which it might be said: "This is his bread-and-butter play, his version of the Lombardi sweep."

I have imitators. But nobody in the neighborhood really comes close to me, from the standpoint of variety and execution, in the consumption of low-calorie beverages.

I usually go to Fresca in the clutch situations, a fact pretty well established on the personalized scouting reports we maintain on the block. But I rarely make the mistake of over-committing myself in the way one of the neighbors does with Diet-Pepsi.

It shows you the difference between the seasoned low-cal drinker and the one just breaking in, whose

future, as Van Brocklin used to say, is all ahead of him.

A can of Fresca will cost you maybe two calories. A can of Diet-Pepsi can't begin to match those statistics although it is no doubt a very admirable liquid of good quality and relatively high food value.

But what has food value got to do with America's Sunday afternoon groaning board? If it did, we'd all be munching Kretschmer's wheat germ. And when was the last time you tried Kretschmer's in a tight ball game?

I mentioned the premium I put on variety at the beverage bar on Sundays. My customary strategy is to open with three cans of Fresca in the refrigerator and a mixture of Tab, Fresca, Brimfull Orange and Dad's Old Fashioned Root Beer in the basement. That way I can improvise in accordance with the game situation. Because consistency is the hallmark of all football success, my preference is to stay with Fresca unless emergencies develop or you quickly establish that Fresca just doesn't have it today.

In this, I liken my technique to that of the Viking Coach, Bud Grant, assessing the performance a couple of years ago of the indomitable wetback, Joe Kapp.

"People couldn't understand it when I pulled Joe after the first four or five series in 1969 at a time when he was having a great season," Bud would recall. "But Joe was one of those guys who telegraphed a bad day very quickly. It wasn't necessarily in things that appeared in the statistics or were always apparent to the fan. But the coach could get the message pretty fast, and there wasn't much of a choice but to relieve Joe as long as there was a capable replacement on the bench."

Borrowing generously from Grant's philosophy, I will not hesitate to shift to Tab if (a) we are trailing by two touchdowns after five minutes or (b) the Fresca simply is not synchronizing on this particular day with the cheddar-spread Melba toast.

I find Tab a good, all-purpose football beverage, nothing really spectacular but a dependable plugger. Brimfull Orange and especially Dad's Old Fashioned Root Beer (just one (1) calorie per can!) are capable of some glittering things in certain clutch situations. I specifically like Dad's when the opposition is going for the bomb and you want something with a minimum of acid and gaseous quantity. I have not tested either one under game conditions for the full four quarters, although this is a possibility I certainly have not ruled out.

My wife's reaction to my Sunday dining itinerary is one of quiet revulsion softened by maternal fear. The woman is afraid I am going to develop scurvy or Artie's Lockjaw or whatever it was the British sailors contracted when they fell short of limes and asparagus. Her pain is aggravated by the fact that my wife is an accomplished cook, a craftsperson of blue ribbon potential. Several times she has lobbied for the chance to make a Sunday afternoon buffet that would meet all standards of minimum subsistence. It would have proteins and enzymes. In spite of these disadvantages, it would still appeal to the football fan.

Accordingly, we struck a deal that both of us were convinced would be dishonored by the end of the first timeout.

I agreed to let her prepare (I volunteered to help with the miscellaneous scullery chores such as peeling and end-cutting) a mobile 12-course menu for one of the Sunday afternoon marathons, the six-hour special.

She would be granted this privilege at least three times during the season.

For her part, my wife would permit me the use of two in-line television sets three times during the season. It was an historic decision, breaking a resolution she had made the day of our engagement. She had grimly observed it for 16 years, dating all the way back to the years when pro football used to collide with Alistair Cooke on Omnibus 90.

As a sporting proposition, my wife said she was willing to accept any reasonable outside suggestion as to menu, that she would not be dictatorial about her own recipes. Her only interest, she maintained, was establishing beyond any serious dispute that it is possible to watch football without acquiring yellow jaundice, canker sores or otherwise brutalizing the institution of eating.

She agreed to abide by the recommendations of

a peer, a woman of civility who could be counted upon to hold her pots steady.

The mutually acceptable consultant was Ms. Beverly Kees, the editor of a special weekly food supplement in the Minneapolis Star called Taste. Ms. Kees' selection was a stroke of brilliance. In addition to being a competent journalist and food authority, Ms. Kees had the virtue of being largely ignorant about football. This meant she was not likely to get all strung out worrying about matching the right kind of salad dressing with the down-and-distance situation on the field, a mistake often made by cooks who press on Sunday afternoon.

Well, Ms. Kees produced a menu. It was tested, under conditions of supersecrecy seldom equaled in the modern era of matinee munching. Actually, matinee is a misnomer. The date chosen was none other than New Year's Day of 1972. The occasion was not a pro football six-hour special at all but the Armageddon of all football seasons, the college bowl games that usually begin with 6 o'clock mass in the morning and end at bar-closing time in Miami.

Because this was a controlled experiment, we agreed to limit the air time to approximately eight hours. This would compare with the most gruelling of pro football Sundays, which are not always pro football's exclusively but very often are piggy-backed by the National Hockey League at night.

We spread the food over three games beginning with Texas-Penn State in the Cotton Bowl, continuing through Michigan-Stanford in the Rose Bowl and concluding with Nebraska-Alabama in the Orange Bowl at night.

Let me end the suspense immediately.

The 12-course buffet was a five-gong, gold-star, unparalleled sensation.

I am urging it on the American public without hesitation, not only as a return to an abandoned old grace of dignity-at-table but as a possible salvation of the nation's health.

Does it take work?

There are millions of American women who would vault at the chance to perform this kind of work if it means a return to sanity in the living room and the general gastronomic overhaul of their husbands. It is creative. It is exciting. And it may mean an end to those ~~goddamned~~ potato chip crumbs on the rug.

Is it expensive?

Certainly no more expensive than the Super Elephantine Bag of Frito-Lays, a pony of beer, and two Alka Seltzer.

Does it take time?

No more than the average light dinner. It can be handled in easy stages — some of it the night before, and some of it during the half-hour countdown to kickoff, which is easily the dreariest half-hour in American television.

I insist you try it at least two or three times during the season. It may save your marriage. It may save the old man's lower tract. And it just may save America from Bad Teeth and Loose Gums. In a moment I will provide recipes.

1. Boka Ditos de Guatemala — an appetizer served in front of the television.
2. Belgian Beer Stew — served on a TV tray.
3. Lena's rolls — on TV tray.
4. Tossed salad with French dressing — TV tray.
5. Dry red wine or beer, or Fresca (or Dad's Old Fashioned if the crisis starts early) — on TV tray.
6. Orange sherbet served in a hollowed orange — TV tray.
7. Coffee — TV tray and then in warmer on a buffet table.
8. Swedish nuts — buffet.
9. Beer and cheese wafers — buffet.
10. Vegetables (raw) and dill dip — buffet.
11. Beef roll-ups (sandwiches) — buffet.
12. Platter of brownies, cookies — buffet.

Bear in mind now that the foregoing is not prepared for the Third Army's two weeks maneuvers but for six to eight hours of television football, which can be even more strenuous. Obviously it is not intended for solo performances. This is family-type fare, although it certainly is not out of place for couples.

The appetizers lead off, usually around 11:30 or 12, followed by a TV tray lunch of salad and stew, then by some civilized snacks accompanied by beverage of choice to stave off the mid-afternoon slump and later vegetables, nuts, a sandwich and cookies to roll back the final assaults of hunger as twilight approaches.

In this way the fans will have been accorded their regular two squares by a kind of conveyor belt method. The demands of good taste will have been met. There is a minimum of sweeping and mopping up — and there may even be a few leftovers for the Monday night game.

I promised recipes. For the tossed salad, cookies, beverage, vegetables, coffee and orange sherbet you will be happy to be on your own and need no sideline call from us, although Ms. Kees has provided a footbally French dressing for the salad.

The advantage of the boka ditos is that they are served hot. This gives the assembled football zealots a high-octane launch into the perilous unknown of Sunday afternoon.

BOKA DITO DE GUATEMALA

*1/2 cup grated Romano
 cheese
1 cup mayonnaise
1/2 cup grated
 Parmesan cheese*

*Small onions, sliced
 wafer thin
Thin sliced bread or
 unflavored crackers
Paprika*

Mix cheeses and mayonnaise. Store in refrigerator until ready to prepare appetizers. Cut thin bread into squares, trimming crusts. Spread with cheese mixture. Top with thin slice of onion. Sprinkle with paprika. Broil until bread is lightly toasted and cheese heated thoroughly. Serve hot.

The Belgian beer stew is reputed to be the ultimate in manly-type lunch or dinner cuisine, ranking right up there with bulls' intimates, the old specialty of Jackson Hole, Wyoming before the tourists arrived. Ms. Kees suggests that while it takes a few hours to cook, it is just made for the type of chef who lives by the creed: "Let's toss in a bunch of this and see what happens." So, feel free to improvise. Don't, however, substitute gin for the scotch whisky.

BELGIAN BEER STEW

3 lb. chuck roast	2 tsp. sugar
1 smoked ham hock	2 tbsp. parsley flakes
1/2 cup oil	Pinch each marjoram,
2-1/2 tsp. salt	thyme and rosemary
1 large onion, thinly	1 clove garlic,
sliced (approx. 1-1/2	chopped fine
cups)	4 carrots, cut in 1-inch
3 tbsp. flour	pieces
Beer, room temperature	3/4 cup walnuts
2 beef bouillon cubes	2 tbsp. red wine
1 cup boiling water	vinegar
1/2 tsp. black pepper	2 tbsp. scotch whisky

Cut beef into 1x2-inch strips. Remove ham from bone and cut in 1/2-inch cubes. Brown beef and ham in oil in large skillet. Lift meat out of oil, sprinkle with 1 tsp. salt and set aside. Brown onions in same oil, then set aside in another dish. Dissolve bouillon cubes in boiling water and let cool. Drain off and reserve all but 3 tbsp. oil in skillet. Stir flour into oil to make a light brown roux. Gradually add 1-1/2 cups beer, stirring until mixture boils. Add bouillon, rest of salt, pepper, sugar, herbs and garlic.

Alternate layers of meat, onions and carrots in a large casserole. Add sauce and enough more beer to cover meat. Cover and cook in a 300-degree oven for 2-1/2 hours. Check occasionally and add beer as needed.

Shortly before stew is ready, saute walnuts in reserved oil. It takes only a couple minutes to get them crisp so watch them carefully. They scorch easily. Add them to stew. Just before serving, add vinegar and scotch. Serves 8.

The perfect satellites for the beer stew are Lena's Rolls, allegedly pioneered by lumberjack chefs among the fabled piece-cutters of the northeastern Minnesota muskeg swamps.

LENA'S ROLLS

1-3/4 cups milk	*1/3 cup sugar*
1/2 cup shortening	*1 egg, slightly beaten*
1 pkg. dry yeast	*1 tsp. salt*
1/4 cup lukewarm water	*6 cups flour*

Scald milk. Add shortening and let milk cool to lukewarm. Dissolve yeast in warm water. Add sugar and yeast to milk, then egg, salt and flour. Turn dough out onto floured board and knead until elastic. Shape into a ball and place in a greased bowl. Let rise, covered, in a warm place until double in bulk. Punch dough down. Divide in half. Divide each half into 12 balls. Grease two bread pans. Flatten each ball and roll it up tightly into a roll to fit the width of the pans. Place 12 rolls closely side by side in each pan and let rise until nearly double in bulk. Bake in a preheated 400-degree oven about 25 minutes or until loaf sounds hollow when tapped on the bottom. When cool, the bread can be broken into 12 "slices" by hand.

The dressing for the TV tray has an autumnal zing and will blend in terms of color texture if the Kansas City Chiefs happen to be on television.

FRENCH DRESSING

1/2 cup vegetable oil	*1/2 tsp. salt*
2 tbsp. vinegar	*1/4 tsp. paprika*
2 tbsp. lemon juice	*1/4 tsp. dry mustard*

Find a jar with a tight-fitting cover. Measure all ingredients into the jar. Screw cover on securely and shake well. Keep covered jar of dressing in the refrigerator. Shake dressing again to mix just before using. Makes 3/4 cup.

It is not necessary to wait until a day when the field goal kicker Jan Stenerud is performing to try out the Swedish nuts. Nor do you have to be a Swede to make or enjoy Swedish nuts. Their appeal is universal except among the stadium fans in Baltimore, who like to munch sunflower seeds and shower the husks on visiting players.

SWEDISH NUTS

2 egg whites   1 lb. salted nuts
1 cup sugar   6 tbsp. butter

Beat egg whites until stiff peaks form. Add sugar and beat until it is well blended. Stir in the nuts until all are coated with the egg whites. Melt butter in a large, shallow pan; spread nuts on the butter and bake 30 minutes at 325 degrees, stirring every 10 minutes. Let cool in pan. Makes 2-1/2 - 3 cups candy-coated nuts.

Dill dip will be welcomed by the calorie-conscious as well as by particular people preferring piquant pickles.

DILL DIP

1 cup sour cream   1 tsp. Beau Monde
1 cup mayonnaise   seasoning
2 tsp. dill weed   1 tsp. minced onion

Mix all ingredients together. Refrigerate at least 2 hours before serving.

DIET DILL DIP

1 cup cream-style   Dash salt
    cottage cheese   1 tsp. fresh dill
1 tbsp. lemon juice

Put cottage cheese, lemon juice and salt in blender. Cover and blend at low speed about 4 minutes, or until smooth. Pour into serving dish. Sprinkle with dill. Garnish with carrot slices. Serve with raw vegetables or chips. Makes about 1 cup.

While run-of-the-mill snackers might be favoring a heartburn condition going into the Sunday afternoon stretch run, the authentic pros — or at least the ones on Ms. Kees' 12-course special — will now be yearning for beef and onion rolls. This one will be applauded by horseradish lovers who have been ignored thus far and have been craving some signs of recognition.

BEEF AND ONION ROLLS

4 slices rare roast beef *1 tsp. horseradish sauce*
1 onion, sliced *1/4 cup softened butter*
2 tbsp. butter *4 hot dog buns*

Saute the onion in 2 tbsp. butter and drain on paper towel. Spread the onion on the slices of roast beef and roll up. Combine the horseradish with the softened butter and spread on the four buns. Put a beef roll in each bun, wrap well in plastic wrap and refrigerate to chill well before taking to a picnic. Makes four sandwiches.

Horseradish sauce, or a milder mixture of 1/2 cup mayonnaise and 2 to 3 tbsp. horseradish sauce, makes a good topping for Beef and Onion Rolls.

The beer-and-cheese wafers can come practically anywhere during the siege but might very well be used by more methodical fans during the crucial tapering-off or withdrawal period of The Scoreboard Show. The wafers have been given an exacting test in the Kansas City parking lot of Metropolitan Stadium during a Viking-Packer game, and got more cheers than the combined offenses of both teams.

BEER AND CHEESE WAFERS

1 lb. grated Cheddar cheese	*1/4 tsp. Worcestershire sauce*
1/4 lb. butter	*1-1/2 cups sifted flour*
1/3 cup beer	*1/2 tsp. salt*
	1/8 tsp. dry mustard

Let cheese and butter soften at room temperature. Mix with a wooden spoon or your hands until fairly smooth. Work in the beer and Worcestershire sauce. Sift together flour, salt and dry mustard and add to cheese mixture. The mixture will be hard, but blend thoroughly. Shape mixture into a roll 2 inches in diameter and about 2 feet long. Wrap in foil or plastic wrap and chill. With a sharp knife, cut roll into slices 1/8 inch thick. Place on ungreased cookie sheets. Salt lightly. Bake at 400 degrees about 8 minutes, until lightly browned. Serve as a snack or with French onion soup or consomme.

Do I hear some protests from the timid here? There is some grog in the cookery. Rest easily. It is the essence of the kitchen art. Not all gourmets sail on French liners. Some like the five-man line.

There is just too ~~damned~~ much food, you say? Nonsense. Never overlook the risk of late-afternoon drop-ins, one of the standing dreads of American society since the advent of pro football television.

When people run out in their own pantry, they start foraging across the street. Ms. Kees' 12-courser is an absolute defense against this kind of unwarranted invasion.

So do it.

But just as a final precaution, keep a bag of taco-flavored Doritos in the cupboard.

Blondes, Too, Can Avoid Mousetraps

It is pretty well documented by the Bureau of Census that not all women who watch football are protective housewives, belligerent grandmothers or Bathroom Annies.

Some of them are warm-breathed, feverishly eligible bachelor girls.

It is in the nature of bachelor girls to want to meet bachelor boys. This is all the more true if the sturdy fledgling is a tight end who makes 30 grand a year and demonstrates his virility in front of 50 million people each week by shaving without water, using only a rusty lawnmower blade.

There is a popular suspicion around the suburban apartment labyrinths and stew-zoos that pro football players are not entirely inaccessible, especially if approached by blondes, brunettes or redheads.

Evidence to support this notion is impressive. Several of the athletes have made it public as a form of civic service. The most prominent of these is Joe Namath.

Joe confesses being impaled on a dilemma for years. His instincts for modesty clash with his impatience. Thus it has been a trial for Joe to face life knowing he is somewhat inhibited by the basic requirements of sleep. This has given rise the earnest confession:

"I can't wait to get up in the morning because I get better looking every day."

There must be days when Joe is just overwhelmed with eagerness to rush out of bed.

Joe's widely advertising feats by candlelight, and the obvious magnetism he exerts on the love-famished, have turned him into one of the heroic folk figures of his time. As such he is cast in the role of a man harried and driven to the point of collapse by regiments of aspiring lovers. But through it all he remains steadfast enough to defend the solitude of his humble hearth. And he is resilient enough the next day — after all that back-to-the-wall exertion — to make it to the practice field.

Joe's statistics in this league are formidable. They certainly entitle him to strong consideration on the annual All-Lochinvar team chosen by the American Association of Abdicated Chambermaids.

It may surprise you to learn that among his contemporaries in the whirlpool rooms, Joe ranks as just another good journeyman in this highly competitive field. To his credit, it ought to be said that Joe never claimed the championship. Rosters in the NFL swarm with contenders for such honors. Since it is the intention here to protect the innocent as well as the guilty, none will be identified.

Whatever the ladies' intentions, football writers often are pressured for advice by determined young women on how best to meet the young immortals, and for forbidden information about their private lives.

I admit it is a part of the football-watching cult that deserves attention. But nobody can speak authoritatively about it except the player who has undergone the ordeal of pursuit by the fleet-footed wench.

We will now monitor one of the league leaders, whose career was headed for unparalleled heights until he was drygulched by matrimony. He is still remembered in many of the towns in the league, with no small affection and a certain amount of wonderment.

"I think it's a lot easier for a girl to meet a football player," he relates, "if she knows a friend who knows. Here's what I mean: In every town there are certain places where ballplayers congregate. It's normally close to the hotel because when you've got a 10:30 curfew you like to have a few beers and not have to ride 45 minutes to get back to your hotel, and miss a half an hour of beers.

"The curfew used to be 11 o'clock with most teams. The majority now have 10:30 curfews. Most of the teams used to put the players on their own on Saturday night until curfew. Now a lot of coaches have scheduled meetings for an hour or so after dinner, to sort of get the players attention on the ball game and away from the beer and broads.

"I'm sure the coaches mean well.

"There may be a 7 o'clock meeting for the offense

and 8 o'clock for the defense, but you might have friends on the other platoon and you wait around until it gets to be 9 o'clock or so. You just can't get into much trouble between 9 and 10:30.

"Most guys usually just stick around the hotel now because it's really not worth going out for one hour. Those who are inclined might wade through five or six beers and then it's usually right back to your hotel, where you will occupy yourself very seriously twiddling your thumbs. The penalty or fine obviously keeps everyone in. There is always the temptation to sneak out, and I do not claim complete purity on this, but anyone who knows he is going to play the full game tomorrow ought to be sane about his movements the night before.

"There are exceptions to every rule, right?

"I mentioned that players usually get together at the same places. The word usually gets around among the ladies. Take San Francisco. The North Beach is attractive to a lot of players, especially the younger ones who've heard about it. They have those nude shows that seem pretty far out if the guy spends most of his time in Green Bay or Minneapolis. But the ones who have been in the league for awhile can tell you that you're never going to find much there except for the hustlers. So anybody who has been around any length of time usually goes to a place like the Coal Yard. Don't ask me where it is. It's just a bar. But I have to say it has a lot to recommend it in a down-to-earth sort of way.

"Los Angeles is a strange town. But the spot that everybody heads for there is the Bull 'n Bush. That is the only place I've ever gone, and a man does not give his loyalty cheaply or without good reason.

"I don't make New York much anymore but the big place for ball players there when I was going good was a joint called Mr. Laff's operated by Phil Linz, who got into all that trouble with Yogi Bera for playing the harmonica on the New York Yankees' bus.

"In Baltimore the bar called Sweeney's has been the ballplayers' halfway house for years and still is as far as I know. Cleveland, Detroit, Chicago, Philadelphia — they're not really good towns for a visiting ballplayer because they're spread out and no place has been established as the one that draws the players.

"It's different in the Twin Cities, where most players in the league would rather spend a weekend than any town in the country with the possible exception of San Francisco and Portland, Ore. — which for some reason is unusually productive.

"Players like Minneapolis, St. Paul and even Bloomington because the people are hospitable and recognize you and bend over backward to make you seem welcome. And the chicks seem to go for pro athletes. That plus the fact that there's this place, Duff's in downtown Minneapolis, where a lot of ballplayers spend time and the chicks are aware of it.

"Some of the clubs are staying in the motels out near the stadium, now, but with the possible exception of a new place called Louey's, there isn't one you would feature as a players' hangout.

"I still happen to be a believer that you don't meet many high-class girls in bars. You just don't. You don't sit and buy a chick eight and ten drinks a night and establish any real basis for love lasting through time.

"There are exceptions, obviously. But when you go to a place like Bull 'n Bush you kind of get the feeling that they're there for more or less one reason — to meet a jock and maybe get something going.

"If I were a girl who wanted to meet an athlete I'd find out who knew him. And then I'd just conveniently happen to be there, and have it set up. It's the referred-lead situation, but I think it's probably the best.

"Once in a while a girl will get your telephone number, or get through to you in the hotel if you're on the road, and I say you better be ready if you go that route.

"I remember shortly after my rookie year a chick called me in the off season and said she was a manufacturer's rep for a Chicago sporting goods company. They were thinking about some kind of endorsement and she was in town and would like to make a presentation.

"I happened to be alone in my place at the time,

since my roommate was gone from the apartment. We got to talking on the phone and she disclosed that she was 38-24-36, and I thought that certainly would enhance her presentation.

"When she added that she also had red hair, I told myself 'you certainly can't afford to neglect any business opportunities,' so I casually dropped that it might be a good idea to get together NOW.

"We decided to meet in a restaurant at 10:30 for some drinks. I walked in five minutes late. I remembered we were first supposed to meet in the restaurant reception area. There were two women there. One was pretty old, I mean like 65, on Medicare or social security or something like that. The other one was a big fat one.

"So I think, gee, this redhead is playing the same game I am, so I twisted around to get a pack of cigarettes and I heard someone call me by my first name.

"I turn around and it is the large one.

"I want to just run right out of the door. But I can't. I don't know if she's legitimate or not. So I walk her into the bar, embarrased to death that someone would recognize me. Now understand there are many, many fat women who are lovely human beings. But I had a sort of public image, even though I'm not hung out about images. I take her to the last table way in the back and I order two drinks right now, bang, and chugged them. I just want to say goodbye real fast and get the hell out of there. But I also don't want to be rude, and she still has some of her drink left, so I say 'hey, give me another one' and to make a long story short at 12:30 we're sailing pretty good and we're going to my place to air her presentation.

"By this time she did not seem quite so blobby. In a certain light there after the sixth drink she seemed almost sleek.

"We got to my apartment and I decided that the first thing we should do is to make coffee. I started to put some on and asked about her presentation. But she said she really needed some visual aids for that and maybe she could go back to her motel in the morning to get her kit. This sounded reasonable to me, so I put on some more coffee. She excused herself, saying she would like to freshen up. When she reappeared in the doorway of the kitchen she was completely native, untouched by any fabric whatsoever, and I want to say I was stupefied.

"Maybe I was seeing clearer because of the coffee or maybe it was because she was out of the candlelight. But whatever the reason was, she had the general lines of the Queen Elizabeth, and I don't mean the queen I mean the ship. Her bow loomed all over the shoreline and you could only speculate about the rest.

"At that exact moment I vowed I would not contribute to the corruption of any visiting businesswoman in her moment of weakness, because I just was not that sort of person.

"I told her I was absolutely insistent on this,

"It's funny about the curfew violators. There are more guys who conceal people in their rooms than guys who leave their rooms. So you stash the guest away in a closet until the check is made, and you can sort of take it from there. Naturally, I'm talking and she would thank me for it tomorrow.

"Besides this, I said, I would not be surprised if my roommate came home in five minutes and it would just be awkward all the way around.

"She seemed disappointed to hear this. She wanted to know how I knew my roommate would be home in five minutes.

"'One of the things I have,' I told her, 'is ESP. It doesn't really help me much on the football field, where things happen very quickly, but I find it very reliable off the field.'

"I don't know whether she bought this, but she did leave reluctantly. Afterward I felt very relieved that once more virtue had scored a decisive victory.

"We never did get to her presentation.

"That's actually the way it usually happens. The girls who call you are the ones who don't have a lot to offer or they wouldn't have to call. The good ones always are busy.

"Ten years ago football players on the road did a lot more freelancing. The discipline from a coaching standpoint was a little more relaxed. You have a terrific emphasis on winning today. There's so much money in the game. And there's a lot more money in the fines if they catch you breaking the rules. It used to be $50. Now it's $500 to a thousand.

about my younger, more impulsive days.

"The way the curfew check works, some assistant coach will walk in with a flashlight or tell you to turn out the lights if you've got them on. They usually come in 5 or 15 minutes after the curfew deadline. But there's always a threat of a second one later at night. As a matter of fact that's normally when guys get nailed.

"The favorite — I suppose you'd call them the sanctuaries, if you have offered the lady the shelter of your roof — are the clothes closets and behind the shower curtains. The assistant coach will come in and if he's suspicious he will sometimes make a bee-line for these places. He may even look under the bed, just like in the old movies. Believe it or not, this has been used as a desperation choice, although it really doesn't have much class when you come to think of it.

"You might get some wiseguy coach who will come in and say, 'oh, since when did you start carrying a purse?' And there just isn't much in the way of a snappy comeback you can make to that if the purse is hanging on the door knob. I remember one coach who just stood there until the girl dressed and then walked her out the door.

"There's no telling what happened after that.

"I suppose I was fined three or four times for from $100 to $500 in the years of my unbridled youth. The time I was fined $500 I was completely innocent of any dallying whatsoever. I fell into bad company, our right tackle and outside linebacker. I came in when it was still light. The problem was that it was the next morning.

"Everything is relative about the fines. When you're making $15,000, a fine of $200 is a big crack. When you're making $35,000 or $40,000, what's $500?

"In my good years I always had more fun at training camp than on the road. On most teams, the veterans had a system of covering for each other. They'd pad up the bed to make it look like somebody was sleeping in it. The real exodus usually took place after 1 in the morning. You'd park your car a couple of blocks from the dormitory that night instead of near the dorm. That way, nobody could hear when you started the motor. Sometimes the coaches would notice that, and it got to be a waiting game. I doubt that it's changed any.

"I'm not going to sit here and deny there are certain advantages to being a football player, especially in your formative years. But if you like adventure on the road nowadays, you better have a shrewd sense of timing. Quarterbacks and receivers, I find, are more trained in this sort of thing. Or you better have a great amount of luck."

Not so gifted, unfortunately, was the rookie tackle whose adoring girl friend called him unfailingly at the Vikings training camp in Bemidji years ago. The tenderness of their love was sometimes lost on the coach, Norm Van Brocklin, who ended the day's public announcements in practice one day by declaring:

"And Archie, for Christ sake will you tell your girlfriend not to call you anymore at 2 o'clock in the morning?

"She did it again today. The reason I know is that the call came in on my phone."

One of the things that telephone calls did at 2 in the morning at Bemidji was to violate the Dutchman's lamblike sleep.

The other thing they did was to scare the hell out of the wobbly galahads threading their way by moonlight back to their chambers. It startled them because they had just missed the curfew deadline by three hours.

The World's Biggest Weenie Roast

The money in pro football may be on the 21-inch screen and the glamour may be on the field. But it is in the parking lot where you will find most of the thrills and a good streak of the violence.

The origin of the tailgate phenomenon is loudly disputed by cooking historians. Some contend the first tailgate party in America was the inauguration of Andrew Jackson as president, wherein hundreds of Old Hickory's frontier playmates crashed the White House and ran around on the presidential linen chugging rum and munching sides of beef.

The tradition is perpetuated to this day in Green Bay, Wis., by bands of Packer rooters from Hurley and Rhinelander. They may not match the cider jug revelers in swampy boots but they certainly get no worse than a draw in drams per capita and next-day hangovers.

Other, more precise researchers maintain that the tailgate party — in social enthusaism if nothing else — stems directly from the days when towns-people would gather to witness the annual hangings.

"In some respects," one scholar theorizes, "the doomed folk hero Tom Dooley was to those gatherings what the quarterback Craig Morton is to the crowds in Dallas. Dooley stood a better chance with the hangman than he did with the spectators. Morton has the same feeling when he has to choose between running into Dick Butkus and going out of bounds near the stands."

Other candidates are offered as the tailgate's authentic spiritual ancestor. Some archeologists hold out for the march of Coxey's Army on the nation's capitol in the late 1880s. Among the others prominently mentioned are the Whiskey Rebellion, the California Gold Rush, the six-day fur trappers' charivari in Pierre's Hole, Idaho in 1832 and the Boston Massacre.

Much of this is academic. Baseball wasn't invented by Abner Doubleday, either. And pro football itself does not trace its beginnings to the storming of the Bastille, a belief held by most quarterbacks facing third down in a passing situation.

No matter its origins, the parking lot picnic before and after a football game clearly satisfies the pathological craving of today's football fan to get involved in the action.

It is not enough for the customer to ogle, scream, tear up the goal posts, and lynch the coach.

He seeks a higher calling today.

Tailgating makes him a participant. He can't throw a down-and-out pass nor decapitate the quarterback. But he can charcoal the tar out of three pounds of ground round. In this he is very competitive. Thousands of stadium goers rate the

afternoon a success or failure not from the standpoint of what the hometown goliaths did but
whether they had a better day with the hibachi
than the crowd in the Ford panel next door.

The use of alcoholic beverages at these asphalt
buffets is not entirely unknown. But even the
more resourceful exploits in public drunkenness go
largely unnoticed. They blend naturally into the
background of the more methodical tippling that
separates the good professional tailgater from the
horizontal ones.

Football tailgating actually began with sedate
spreads of sarsaparilla and baked beans under the
apple trees before the Princeton-Harvard games
years ago. Like their moleskinned heroes, the Ivy
League fans were eventually overwhelmed by the
more aggressive Midwesterners.

To this day, the superstars of the tailgating
society — the ones who make up the Black and Blue
Division of the parking lot smorgasbords — are
found in Green Bay, Minnesota, and now Chicago
since the migration of the Bears from Wrigley Field
to Soldier Field.

Geography and local behavior quirks dictate
tailgate practices in the various NFL cities. In
Los Angeles few people get out of bed before the
second quarter, a fact which sharply limits the
popularity of pre-game picnics. Also, most Ange-
linos who are potential tailgaters take their three
screwdrivers with breakfast instead of waiting for
the more formal occasion of parking lot brunch.

In San Francisco tailgating was virtually impossible while the 49ers were playing at Kezar because all of the likely nearby parking lots have been converted into pornography stores.

Also a very strong inhibiting factor was the presence of vast squadrons of overflying seagulls.

"No real competitor," a gnarled die-hard outside the Kezar end zone once told me, "likes to perform under wraps. With all those seagulls, it was the only way to tailgate at Kezar. The worst thing you could bring to a tailgate party at Kezar, for that very reason, was raisin pie. It always led to a credibility gap when you offered some to a friend."

The conditions for Wrigley Field regulars in Chicago, before the move to Soldier Field, were even more dismal than in San Francisco. There was no recognizable parking and the fans' enthusiasm for tailgating was further dimmed by the old suspicion that George Halas required some kind of rebate commission on all hamburger consumed outside the stadium.

In Dallas tailgating is carried on only in rudimentary form alongside the multitudes who gather in the Minnesota and Green Bay lots. This is so because of the actuarial tables.

"The tailgaters that Tabasco sauce didn't get," a local dietician recalled, "sunstroke did."

Baltimore has been unfairly slandered by the charcoal aficionadoes. For a long time the city was not considered seriously as a tailgate hotbed because of the erroneous notion that Baltimore fans

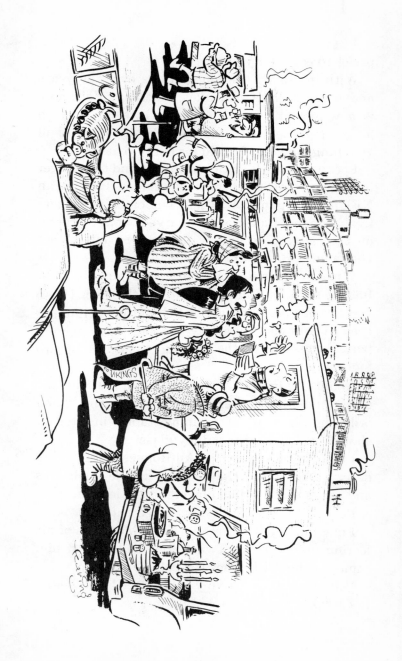

prefer to eat their young.

With improved communications over the years and more tolerant attitudes generally, Baltimore is now looked on with a higher esteem. It is no longer regarded as the Jukes Family of football watching, an honor it held for many years.

Because of the logistics problems and the danger in transporting thousands of seafood fans to an NFL football game with their clam-cracking mallets freshly honed, Baltimore has carved out new ground on the tailgate scene. By far its best efforts are the famed "Baltimore Brunch."

Without question the most exciting pre-game fueling stop for Baltimore fans is the Iron Horse restaurant operated by Bill Pellington. Pellington is a prince of good company now but in his playing period was one of the all-time assassins of pro football.

About Pellington it was said that he was the only middle linebacker in pro football who, when ordering his milk at training table, insisted it should be delivered in a dirty glass.

I used to pick an annual All-Rogues team paying deserved tribute to the 11 most hostile, malicious and anti-social football players in the league.

Pellington invariably was named captain.

I met him a year after he retired. Members of his jeering public in the Twin Cities had mailed him copies of the All-Rogues roll call.

Pelly walked over to my table after I had begun my steak dinner in his restaurant.

"I hope you enjoy the seasoning," he said.

"Yes," I replied, "an exotic flavor. What is it?"

"Extract of strychnine. We keep it in reserve for special guests from Minnesota."

Good old wag, Pelly. I'm sure the only people he really reserved it for were quarterbacks who liked to call the draw play up the middle.

The feature of Pellington's pre-game buffet, aside from vast caches of scrambled eggs, ham, bacon, sausage and gin, was the bus driver.

Customers would be freighted to the stadium from Pellington's Iron Horse aboard four buses. The passengers on three of the buses were routinely boisterous. On the fourth, they were terrified stiff.

I have forgotten the bus driver's name. I think he drove lead tank for Patton through the Ardennes.

His bus, as I recall, would triple the number of rest stops made by the others. You could get by without nerve on this bus but you were finished if you had weak kidneys.

The explanation was the belligerent disposition of the driver. Actually, he was cordial enough in private life. As a bus driver, however, he pursued a fantasy role in which he imagined himself as the logical successor to the great Colt fullback of the 1950s, Alan (The Horse) Ameche.

The difference here was that where Ameche challenged his adversaries with powerful thighs and a hammerlike forearm, the bus driver did it with an eight-foot wide bumper, a reinforced chassis and an excruciating airhorn.

He never went much over the speed limit. But there is no doubt that as he barged into the city limits he saw himself as Ameche, needing three yards to get into the end zone.

Natives in the traffic flow were fully prepared for him and were completely cowed. He would sail into a traffic circle two miles from the stadium and cars would screech to the curb like bantam defensive backs avoiding an end sweep led by six-man interference.

"I'm nothing fancy," the driver would throw back over his shoulder. "I don't maneuver much. I'm more the straightahead type."

Visiting drivers were unaware of this quality. I took one ride on Pellington's bus and counted four cars with Pennsylvania license plates splayed in the middle of the boulevard in the bus' wake. The drivers were chalky and aghast at the wheel.

In Green Bay and in Bloomington, Minn., however, you have the Rose Bowl and Mardi Gras of the tailgate culture. This is only partly explained, and superficially at that, by the parking capacity of the lot. Among my confederates is a Los Angeles newspaperman, Bob Oates, who says he is convinced that in mapping the earth's land mass God plainly envisioned the Midwest prairie as one unbroken stadium parking lot.

Battle-royal brawls have been fought in some Minnesota-Wisconsin border communities over the comparative class and liquor capacities of the tailgate crowds in Green Bay and Bloomington.

My background and loyalties make me vulnerable to a charge of parochialism. In fairness, let me say that Wisconsin tailgaters have a certain grubbing, nosedown stolidity as tailgaters. They are no more than even with Minnesotans under blizzard conditions despite their annual commemoration of the famous Green Bay-Dallas playoff game of January, 1968 which finished with the mercury at 17 below zero and 260 fans welded to the stadium by their backsides.

To the Wisconsin football crowd there is a hallowed quality to this date, one that receives the same triumphant solemnity that the Russians accord the liberation of Leningrad.

Minnesota fans are not stampeded by this performance. True, the temperature got to 17 below. The wind, though, was not much more than a mild breeze, blowing at 13 miles an hour from the northwest.

"No tailgate crowd in the history of professional football has ever equaled Minnesota's magnificent effort in 1970," a Kiester, Minn., season ticket holder reported to a New York television reporter. "On two consecutive home games we tailgated in a windchill of minus 40 and a windchill of minus 38.

"Anybody can do this once.

"It takes a truly championship tailgate crowd to repeat. That has always been the hallmark of greatness."

"Do you see," he was asked, "a dynasty forming here?"

"We don't think in terms of dynasties," he answered. "A lot of things can change from year to year. There are new fans coming up every year. Frostbite takes some of the veteran tailgaters. The weather bureau may come out with a new anemometer. Things like that. I never said we were spectacular. Just consistent. We reflect the team a lot, and even more than the team, the coach."

I would rate the Green Bay tailgate crowd ahead of Minnesota's in roasted bratworst but slightly behind in shish kabob and certainly well behind in marinated meatballs and Polish sausage — which may surprise the neutral observer.

Despite Wisconsin's heralded reserve strength in Polish cooks, it is very likely that northeast Minneapolis, featuring the perennial leader in pierogi and basted spare ribs, Stan Mayslack, actually produces more of star quality.

To its credit, Wisconsin probably has fewer camper collisions in the middle of the parking lot. This happens with some frequency at Metropolitan Stadium in Bloomington. The situation there may have something to do with the camper drivers' popular custom of playing chicken in the northeastern or Baltimore lot.

But if Minnesota's tailgate crowd has one department in which it is clearly superior to Wisconsin it is in a finely-tuned sense of drama, a capacity for the historic happening.

It was in Metropolitan Stadium where the first NFL divisional title game was viewed in its entirety from a 50-foot high snowbank, beyond the stadium walls but with a great angle of sight overlooking the north end zone.

It was also at Metropolitan Stadium where the incomparable Ching Johnson, wearing Viking horns and a Kirk Douglas eyepatch, played host to 350 of his close friends in a semi trailer parked in the Cleveland lot during the Viking-Green Bay game of 1970.

I have to tell you in all modesty that I was part of that glorious assembly. Johnson paid $600 for the required spirits and roughage. The revelers were wedged into the van in a way that reminded you of ten goal line defenses stacked between the five and the ten. For food you had to settle for anything that was passed out head high. All movement except the most essential was banned. I was kissed five times and ate three passing corn beef sandwiches without taking my hands out of my pockets. I did it with peripheral vision.

Some of the group made it to the ball game.

Four who didn't were the musicians, who were attached to one of the walls of the semi and gave out with five minutes to go in the game, the victims of an unknown malady. An ambulance was summoned and a lively quarrel arose over whether they should be sent to the in-patient ward at General Hospital or the detoxification center.

The argument turned out to be irrelevant. The 30 mile an hour northwest wind acted as a tonic, reviving the musicians. They left the parking lot riding atop a Volkswagon, playing The South Hiawatha Avenue Rag.

Despite Ching Johnson's superb showing, however, the most sensational happening still must be credited to a bartender named Bill Caughfey and a receptionist named Caryl Meyer.

Highly motivated Viking partisans, they decided to meet their twain in the Kansas City lot and become the first couple to be married at a tailgate party.

Friends had arranged a New England shore dinner of lobster, baked chicken, sweet corn, baked potatoes, pink Chablis and three kinds of oysters. It was relatively modest fare when measured against the tailgate standards of the 1970s at the Met. But both bride and groom confided they planned to spend the first stage of their honeymoon at halftime in a Winnebago camper rented especially for the occasion.

After the game reporters ignored John Brockington and Carl Eller and rushed to the Winnebago.

"I think Judge Lommen did a tremendous job out there today," the bridegroom said quietly, preferring to ignore his own considerable role. "The Judge's work was the kind easy to overlook in all the excitement.

"That's the trouble with the media. They concentrate on the spectacular things in a parking lot wedding — I mean the pink Chablis, Caryl's pregame preparedness list. Listen. All I did was say 'I do.' It's like going into the end zone when you've got five guys in front of you taking out the defensive line.

"It was the judge who did the bread-and-butter work. A lot of judges might have pressed in those conditions. They might have come into the parking lot emotionally overcharged and therefore ineffective.

"But Judge Lommen never anticipated, never shifted cadence. It was beautiful the way he came up to that 'love, honor and cherish.' There were all kinds of distractions. The Viking band was playing 'Skol, Vikings, Skol' someplace inside the stadium and Paul Flatley was on the radio doing color on somebody's transistor. The whole effect on the ceremony was like Dick Butkus yelling at the quarterback while he's trying to call an audible.

"But the judge just hung in there and said, 'and now the ring, please,' and everything went just like the counsellor said in our Thursday talk.

"The judge even played the wind right. I don't know whether you realize it, but there was a tricky little crossfield breeze coming in just at the downbeat of Lohengrin. So the judge wisely had the rice-throwers move behind the Winnebago and make their ceremonial tosses from there.

"A little thing, yes. But you expect it from a man like the Judge. What it meant was the rice-throwers could go with the wind. This was very gratifying to Caryl and me because four of our best friends were barbecuing some knackwurst in the next parking stall, and it would have been a terrible combination, knackwurst and flying rice."

It never showed in the statistics, but that's the Judge. A team man.

A Snowsuit, Thermos, Bratwurst — and Thee

Throwing out the 1971 Minnesota Vikings, no football team of the modern era has tried to win with a Pop Warner offense.

Similarly, football fans of the 1970s quail at the flimsy preparation and cavalier fatalism their forbears of the 1930s brought to the ballpark.

It is considered reckless and unscientific to attend the ballgame today without first going through a stadium check list as precisely as the pilot examines his own check list before clearance.

Needs and urgencies vary from fan to fan and will be strongly influenced by the weather and the position of the home team in the standings. But the typical ticket buyer will want timely postings on:

1. Wind chill (includes temperature, wind and sometimes the forecaster's zip code).
2. Wind direction at ground level and also, for third deck customers, winds aloft, barometric pressure and oxygen content.
3. Pollen count.
4. Pollution level.
5. Dangers of casual exposure (seasonal) to

pneumonia, sunstroke, Asiatic flu, frostbite, windburn and Dutch elm disease.

6. Most recent servicing of waterproof lubricant for snowmobile suits, official team beanies, and other moving parts.

7. Condition of thermos.

8. Serviceability of Coleman cooker, hibachi, cigarette lighter or other sources of heat; dryness of matches (remembering to save one for the stadium in the fourth quarter in case of second games of the TV double header).

9. Condition of thermos.

10. Availability in car's trunk of tent, sleeping bags and emergency flares to help needy tailgaters who have lost the way between their own car trunk and the back seat.

11. Floor plans and architect's drawings showing locations of stadium rest rooms.

12. Condition of auxiliary thermos.

The watchword of the football goer today, as it is in the corset industry, is adjustability.

The degree to which he masters it is the difference between the plodder and the thoroughbred. Take the matter of drink at the ballyard. Obviously there are millions watching football games who don't drink.

Very few of these, however, watch them in Green Bay, Milwaukee, Minnesota, Kansas City, Denver, St. Louis, Dallas, Houston, San Diego, San Francisco, Los Angeles, Detroit, Chicago, Buffalo, New

York, Pittsburgh, Philadelphia, Boston, Miami, Atlanta, New Orleans, Cincinnati, Cleveland and Washington.

There is very little drinking at the stadium in Baltimore. Most of the fans there already are right at the allowable limits when the gates open.

The day has vanished when the fan could show up with a hip flask or a six-pack of beer and hope to attain any kind of esthetic satisfaction. In preparing his thermos today he has to allow for weather conditions, the rated capacity of his neighbors in Section 34 and the expected number of play stoppages based on past performance.

The bartenders' ready list that follows is not offered in any binding, arbitrary spirit. Look on it as a guide if you are confused by the complexities of life in the grandstand in the 1970s.

The recipes are standard in many cases but are attributable here to a professional bartender and longtime Minneapolis pro football buff, Rick Sorensen of the Little Wagon Bar's Sunday Swashbucklers, a noisy bleacher group of some local notoriety.

Hot Bloody Mary — 1-1/2 oz. vodka, 3 drops Tabasco, 4 drops Worcestershire sauce, 1 oz. horse radish. Stir.

Effective at temperatures down to 20 below and considered de riguer for games involving the Bears, Lions, Vikings, Packers and Buffalo. Early season users will want to apply the horse radish carefully, or possibly save it for neighbors who are cooking braised ribs today.

Screwdriver — 1-1/2 oz. vodka, 3 oz. orange juice. Stir.

This is the standard, pro-type fare, useable under most weather conditions. It is ideal for undercover imbibers who wish to pour it into an empty orange soda pop bottle to decoy the church parson and his wife sitting a row down. This strategy often breaks down when the parson turns and asks if you might need something to strengthen your screwdriver.

Hot Brandy, Rum, or Bourbon — 1-1/2 oz. of brandy, rum or bourbon, 1/2 oz. of simple syrup or sugar, 3 oz. of hot water. Stir well. Float nutmeg on top and add twist of lemon.

A festive-type football drink usually reserved for December 27th playoffs in a snowstorm. A favorite of playful fans who like to put the hot brandy in a miniature barrel looped tastefully around the wife's neck.

Coffee Kanuke — 1 oz. brandy, 1 oz. Kahlua, 2 oz. coffee. Stir well or shake if in container.

This is a popular liqueur with an extremely swift warming action, recommended for those likely to faint at the sight of three straight interceptions.

Harvey Wallbanger — 1-1/2 oz. vodka, 1 oz. Galliano, 5 oz. orange juice.

Expensive but very toney, usually favored by noisy, self-confident extroverts who know what the next play is going to be every time. Not to be confused with noisy, self-confident extroverts who think they know the next play. Show me the fan who stands up and yells, "all right, they're all set up for the slip screen to this side," and I'll show you a Wallbanger fan.

Black Russian — 2-1/2 oz. vodka, 1 oz. Kahlua. Stir. Best on rocks.

The variation on this, though, and much more popular at the stadium is:

Poor Man's Black Russian — 1 oz. vodka, 1 oz. blackberry brandy. Stir or blend. Drink on the rocks or straight.

This is not only less expensive than the stock Black Russian but much more versatile, allowing the fan the same kind of choice the coach gives his option quarterback. You can go either way, stir or blend, rocks or straight, depending on the game situation. This one seldom makes the gourmet all-pro lists but it is a workhorse in most ballparks, one the sportswriters used to call a journeyman. For cold weather fans, it comes close to being prescription stuff.

Stinger — 2-1/2 oz. brandy, 1 oz. white creme de menthe. Stir or blend.

Bluntly, I consider it an imposter at the football game. This is primarily the drink of the faint-

hearted, the ones who watch the home games in bars equipped with 5,000 foot antennae to nab the signal from Mason City or Chapultepec.

Slo-Screw — This is one that can be misunderstood. It is not intended for unpracticed drinkers but should only be attempted by those who are seasoned and will not be taken in by this drink's casual exterior. 1-1/2 oz. slo-gin, 3 oz. orange juice. Stir.

For exhibition games only.

Aspen Glow — 1 oz. vodka, 1 oz. gin, 1 oz. rum, 1 oz. tequilla, 1 oz. Triple Sec, 2 oz. Galliano, 4 oz. orange juice. Blend or shake well.

Contrary to your first assumption, this has not been prepared for ALL of Section 34 but for single, individual, free-floating fans. Because of the moves required by the consumer simply to stay vertical, this drink is favored by those who see themselves as split ends — not the tight ends as you might expect. According to legend, Joe Kapp is the one NFL player known to have taken an Aspen Glow in the off-season and functioned more lucidly afterwards than before.

Some of these may be found in the parking lots, where the tailgating legions are active at their merry forges. This I regret. The cocktail is a high megaton type of football beverage. It should be last-resort stuff, for use in the crash of action. In some places it is technically illegal to bring grog into the stadium. C'est le guerre. It is also technically illegal for football clubs to force their customers to pay for exhibition games on their season tickets. It's a standoff.

But while a highball or beer at the tailgate banquet is acceptable, the mixed stuff is mainly medicinal, especially in the glacial belt where winter football begins on Columbus Day.

From tailgaters, you look for a little more style, some urbanity in beverage selection, don't you? This is why you have to be impressed with the newlyweds who chose Chablis instead of Boone's Farm apple wine — which is rapturously acclaimed at the rock festivals. And since there is such a thing as style on the parking pavements, how about a good, all-purpose, multi-offense kind of tailgate menu that should be strong against all opposition?

It has been tested by the previously introduced Ms. Kees and some exuberant members of one of the suburban Odd Fellows organization. They all praise its sturdiness, practicality and ability to withstand high surface winds.

The entree is Beerbecued Steak, preceded by hot spiced cider and served with beer or dry red wine as the beverages; also French bread, tossed salad or fresh vegetables, chips or shoestring potatoes, coffee and/or Rose's Hot Chocolate and grasshopper bars frosted in the pan.

In spite of its impressive dimensions, the menu requires very little charging around at serving time. Last-minute bravado is for the showy tail-gaters in any case, not the working pros.

What the cook does is to tenderize a chuck roast by putting it in marinade before leaving for the parking lot. So, while the tribes are waiting for the steak to cook on the charcoal grill or hibachi, they can warm themselves with the cider if it's cool outdoors, or warm themselves with the cider if it's warm outdoors. The punch can be made at home and brought to the stadium in vacuum jugs, or stirred up in a pot over the charcoal.

The effective tailgater is nothing if not resource-ful. Tarkenton would have made the Tailgate Hall of Fame. Who else could keep a roast, a tray of goulash, a platter of scrambled eggs and a pan of grits going at the same time — in the same direction?

I mentioned the multiple menu. This makes it truly the menu of the 1970s, as Hank Stram might call it. The punch, for example, is drawn from the generally close-to-the-vest repertory of Letha Booth and the Colonial Williamsburg Staff.

HOT SPICED PUNCH

1 qt. apple cider *1 tsp. nutmeg*
3 cinnamon sticks *1 tsp. whole cloves*
4 tbsp. lemon juice

Simmer cider, cinnamon sticks and lemon juice for 15 minutes. Tie nutmeg and cloves in a small cheesecloth bag and put into simmering cider long enough to give the desired taste. Serves 8.

It's possible you might accuse Beerbecue Steak devotees of sectionalism — bringing in the homely, stubborn and straightforward qualities usually pinned on the cornfed midwesterner. I consider this a bad-mouth on both the midwesterner and Beerbecue Steak. In both you are bound to find flashes of inspiration and a latent flavor of worldliness. Don't, however, overdo the chopped onion and garlic. If you do, and you live in the midwest, you are going to blow the images of both the midwesterner and the Beerbecue Steak.

BEERBECUE STEAK

1 chuck roast, 2 inches thick
Meat tenderizer
1/4 cup oil
1 small onion, chopped
1 clove garlic, chopped
6 tbsp. lemon juice
2 cups beer
2 cups chili sauce
1 tbsp. Worcestershire sauce
1 tsp. salt

Slash fatty edge of steak; sprinkle both sides with meat tenderizer; let stand 1 hour. Heat oil and saute onion and garlic until soft. Add lemon juice, beer, chili sauce, Worcestershire and salt. Cook over medium heat until sauce bubbles. Place steak in a shallow pan and cover both sides with sauce. Let stand for at least an hour. When ready to cook, remove steak and place on grill about 6 inches above gray-hot coals. Broil about 20 minutes on each side, brushing with reserved sauce several times. Heat remaining sauce and serve with steak cut in thin slices. Serves 8.

The French bread suggested for this menu is the traditional whole loaf sliced and buttered with garlic butter, sprinkled with Parmesan cheese and heated in foil over the charcoal.

By way of proving you don't have to leave the colonies to go continental, how about this garlic-dappled Italian dressing if you choose tossed salad instead of fresh vegetables?

ITALIAN DRESSING

1/2 tsp. oregano leaves
1 tsp. salt
Dash white pepper
Dash cayenne
1/8 tsp. garlic powder
1/4 tsp. dry mustard

1 tsp. minced onion
1/2 tsp. chopped chives
1/2 tsp. chopped
   parsley or flakes
1/2 tsp. sugar
1/2 cup wine vinegar
1 cup olive oil

Combine all ingredients and shake. Refrigerate at least 1 hour.

On the other hand, the more robust — possibly fixing their aggressions on the vegetable platter — may want to do some double-action crunching in anticipation of the arrival of the Rams' halfbacks. You are almost sure to get satisfaction out of this shrimp dip.

SHRIMP DIP

12 oz. cream cheese
2 cans broken shrimp
   pieces
2 tsp. lemon juice

1/8 tsp. Worcestershire
   sauce
1/8 tsp. garlic powder
   or to taste

2 tsp. minced onion   *Salt and pepper to*
Dash chili powder   *taste*

Combine ingredients and refrigerate overnight. Serve with sliced white radishes, cucumbers, raw cauliflower buds, cherry tomatoes and carrots, celery and green pepper sticks.

Despite the determined propaganda of the beer, Bourbon and Beefeater agents, the use of coffee and hot chocolate has not been banned at football games. An otherwise anonymous tailgater named Rose produced this recipe for hot chocolate. It is guaranteed, she says, to be messless.

ROSE'S HOT CHOCOLATE MIX

1 (25.6-oz.) box   *1 (6-oz.) jar non-dairy*
* powdered milk*   * creamer*
1 (1 lb.) box chocolate   *1 cup sugar*
* drink mix*

Mix well and store in a tightly closed container. (It all fits into a 3-pound coffee tin.) To make 1 cup hot chocolate, put 3 to 4 tbsp. mix into a cup and add hot, boiling water. Makes one cup hot chocolate instantly.

Tailgate cooks who make the varsity at Minnesota's Metropolitan Stadium, which is nationally respected as the Super Bowl of football cooking, invariably are tigers on desserts. The reasoning here is that almost anybody can throw on a steak, swab a little garnish on it, and come out looking like Antoine. The desserts usually separate the cooks from the coal-tenders. This recipe for grass-hopper bars has been a **regular** for years, warding off the challenge of some of its flashier but less durable rivals.

Grasshopper Bars — a crunchy cookie base under a thick cream topped with a minty green glaze — look special and are easy to prepare.

GRASSHOPPER BARS

3/4 cup butter
3/4 cup confectioners'
* sugar*
1 tbsp. light cream
1/2 tsp. baking powder
3-4 drops green food
* coloring*
1/4 tsp. mint flavoring
1-1/2 cups flour

For topping:
1/4 cup butter
1 (3-oz.) pkg. cream
* cheese*
4 cups confectioners'
* sugar*
1/4 tsp. salt
1/4 tsp. mint flavoring
3-4 tbsp. light cream
Green food coloring

Cream first three ingredients and add baking powder, green food coloring and mint flavoring. When blended, mix in flour. Pat dough out in bottom on an ungreased 13x9-inch pan. Bake at 325 degrees 25-30 minutes, until lightly browned. Cool slightly. Soften remaining butter and cream cheese. Whip together and add confectioners' sugar, salt, mint flavoring and enough light cream to make spreading consistency. Reserve 1/2 cup and spread the rest over the cookie base. To reserved 1/2 cup add a little green food coloring and enough cream to make the consistency of glaze. Spread glaze over white filling. Cut into bars.

Food and booze at the ballpark, while no doubt convenient, are dim consolation if you fumble the real key to survival in American football, the clothes rack.

In the tropical reaches of the National Football League this presents no special challenges. An exception is Atlanta, where the field drainage is terrible and it is literally possible for customers in the first 10 rows to drown in games where there are a lot of timeouts.

Houston fans immersed in the Astrodome are relatively safe the year round, although there is always a chance of asphyxiation if the air conditioning goes out. New Orleans and Miami have minor problems with hurricanes; in Los Angeles it is possible to choke to death in calm air; San Diego offers an original problem in tidal waves. In San Francisco there is always a threat of the fan being assaulted by vindictive seagulls.

In most of these towns, however, the outdoor equipment is pretty standardized. For the bona fide dilemmas you have to look elsewhere. In Minnesota last year, there was a temperature differential of 88 degrees between the hottest day (an August exhibition) and the coldest (anything after November 15).

Midwesterners naturally are at a strong advantage over easterners in the purely mathematical chances of surviving winter football, which takes in roughly half of the schedule. Snowmobile suits are staple parts of the Central Division fan's wardrobe. People go dancing in snowmobile suits; they also go to the concert, church and bingo game. They shop in them, shovel in them and some even make love in them — the ultimate faith in the dependability of the American zipper.

And yet nobody outside of Moose Jaw, Sask., would seriously go into a football season putting all of his sartorial eggs in the snowmobile suit.

"You really ought to break the season into thirds," we are advised by one of the world's leading authorities on foul weather garments. This is Wally Clausen, a representative of the Eddie Bauer outfitting firm and a man who is assailed each November by panic-driven football fans who have just heard the five-day forecast and are afraid to trust last year's long johns.

"All you have to worry about in the early season," he says, "is just keeping dry. So you should take some light rainwear and maybe some wool to absorb the moisture.

"If you are likely to be active, put this fishnet underwear beneath what you normally wear as an undergarment. It will have the effect of transferring the body moisture to the outer garment.

"One of the things that's coming in big now for September-October football is the two-piece warmup suit, a nylon outfit you see joggers wearing. It costs only $23 and makes the wearer look very athletic and classy but can be slipped on and off very easily. If you're going to slip it off at the ballpark for something else, make sure you've got something underneath. You will want to have some wool, of course, plus rain gear.

"The crisis comes in the winter. The snowmobile suit is good, but it might need quite a few supplements, plus it is a terrible problem for some users with erratic plumbing habits."

Winter football watchers break down into two categories. There is the tough-it-out school, whose disciples argue they have lived here all their lives and see no reason why they have to put on Himalayan expedition boots to watch a ball game.

Some of these do not re-appear again until May, when they are disinterred from the second deck during the spring thaw.

The others pretty much belong to the empty-the-attic school. Its practitioners will insist on hauling to the stadium everything in the house that is not at the laundry, over the windows or under quarantine.

"A kind of underwear that's coming back," Clausen revealed, "is what they call the itchy-scratchy wool long johns, blazing red with a drop-seat. For stockings you will want one lightweight pair under a set of heavy wools, and for boots anything felt-lined. Over the underwear you want something heavy and wool, a Pendleton or ski sweater, and over that a heavy jacket, coat or warmup, possibly down-filled. Remember, you can always take stuff off. But there's nothing you can

do if you start getting cold, except maybe shang-
hai some guy on his way to the coffee stand at
half. A hood or parka or some kind of head and
ear covering is mandatory and many are now
wearing face masks. For mittens, something wool
or down-filled, with retractable liners, and over
all of this a waterproof cape if it's raining or
snowing."

He looked as though he had forgotten something.

"Also," he said, "pray for a lot of ground plays.
They eat up the clock."

Does all of this work? Two years ago the sensa-
tions of the Met Stadium were a couple from Duluth
in tails and gown. There in the parking lot for a
September game they unfurled an immaculate
linen, draped it over a table, surmounted it with
two candelabra and looked soulfully at each other
in the soft twilight as a valet served pheasant
under glass and the record player caressed the
scene with Rachmaninoff's Concerto No. 2.

The skeptics said they could never repeat.

They did, last December, the entire scene. There
was one variation. Instead of a tuxedo and chiffon
gown they wore matching snowmobile suits, a
Polaris for Her and an Arctic Cat for Him.

Not All of Them are Greek Gods

The faces of professional football players today adorn bottle caps, bedroom walls, chewing gum cards, sauna bath parlors and convent retreats.

They are lionized and romanticized, compared with Ben Hur, Samson and Sir Launcelot. They are quoted so often and faithfully that they have now become the only entertainers in America who can belch in a post-game interview and wake up the next day to see it converted into an eight-column headline.

This is by and large a pity and a hornswoggling of the American public. The chromium glamor tends to gild all of the jocks impartially — the superstars, the plughorses and the Pagliacios. It is a shame, because America deserves to know more about the sad, floppy-shoe obscurities who surface only when the camera gets focused on the wrong guy or the Pittsburgh Steelers accidentally show up on televison.

The Pittsburgh Steelers are brought up here for no defensible reason except that from freshly uncovered manuscripts, found floating in battered beer kegs on the Monongahela, they are slowly emerging as one of the heroic miscarriages in the history of show business.

It used to be said the Steelers of the 1960s were the one team in the NFL committed to a policy of de-emphasizing football.

"This is a libel," scoffed one of its most devout although least legendary alumni, linebacker John Campbell.

"I do think it's fair to say that the Steelers were the only team in the league to go through a whole training camp season without winning an intra-squad game."

John Campbell is now honorably retired from pro football, having spent two years with Van Brocklin and four with the Steelers. There are few if any living people qualified to wear this rare combination of campaign ribbons. To understand how much genuine wonderment it produces at the player reunions, imagine an infantryman who took part in the Normandy Invasion, Guadalcanal, the Battle of the Bulge, Iwo Jima, Anzio Beach and the mess call at Fort Riley.

The Steelers didn't win many games. When you look it up you find out they actually didn't make many first downs. The most exciting things the Steelers did offensively was to kick extra points, exciting because suspense would always clutch the Steeler fans: Does Booth Lustig kick the ball this time or does he kick the guy who is holding the ball?

The Steelers seemed to constitute their own league. The Lord knows they didn't belong in the other. Seldom has mediocrity been pursued with such fortitude and ingenuity.

And yet John Campbell's devotion to that dark-starred clan of free booters, roustabouts and vaude-villians is deep and invincible.

"In case the fan ever gets the idea that all pro football runs smoothly and everybody is a matinee god," John Campbell tells us now from the shelter of his brokerage office in Minneapolis, "the Steelers were living proof that the fan doesn't know what the hell he's talking about.

"I came to the Steelers from Baltimore as a sort of carom shot that originated with the Vikings. The Steelers were just fantastic people. We played a game in Cleveland on Saturday night where they introduced the teams before 80,000 people. You ran across the baseball diamond onto the field. They introduced Preston Carpenter of our group. He came sailing out of the runway, rounded first and slid into second with the prettiest hook slide they ever saw in Cleveland. He got up, dusted himself off and doffed his helmet to the crowd, which roared and screamed for him to steal third.

"The Steelers were the last great collection of bar-fighting hell-raising football players to survive Madison Avenue. The only thing we didn't do was pass the hat during the game. It was that type of outfit. Anytime you put Bobby Layne on the staff with Buddy Parker, you are going to have prob-lems. The guys would sit there and fight. And they'd go out and have drinks together. You would see one of your teammates come back and his face would look like nine miles of bad road, and he'd been in a fight with one of his buddies over some bimbo in Rhode Island.

"You can't believe the pep talk Parker gave us one game. We were playing the 49ers at Brown University. It's an exhibition, on national television. Parker is standing there, taking down half a cigarette in one drag, putting his nose in the fork of fingers when he inhaled the cigarette — the classic Parker Style. He looks around the locker room and you can see he's trying to figure out a way to trade the whole goddamned team. And he says 'okay, I want you to see if you can go out there for all of your millions of TV fans without tripping over your clumsy feet. And if you bastards don't show me something it's going to be just too bad.' That was it. That was the pep talk. I looked at Charlie Bradshaw, and I said 'I don't know when I've been this stirred up about a game.'

"We went out and they just buried us. They fired Parker a few hours later, just before he was about to get rid of all 40 ballplayers.

"I mentioned Charlie Bradshaw, a great, decent guy. He must have gone 6 foot 9 and 250. But he always used to have this clean uniform. He said he wasn't helping anybody rolling around in the mud. A couple of the guys didn't see that because they figure you got to be grubby looking to play well. But Charlie had the right idea. We used to call him Mr. Clean or The White Rabbit. He was in the bar one day drinking buttermilk and this guy comes in and says, 'hey Charlie, how you doing?' and knocks over his buttermilk. Charlie ordered another one. The guy comes back a few minutes later on his way from the men's room and says, 'well, I see you're still on the stuff,' and he knocks it over again.

"Charlie didn't say a word. He just picked him up and threw him out the window. I don't mean he threw him out the open window. I mean he threw him through the WINDOW. The first thing the guy hit was a fire hydrant and the last we heard about him he was assigned to Ward 3.

"It didn't take much of an excuse to start a celebration with the Steelers. I remember one year we opened the season by kicking off to the Chicago Bears. The guy caught the ball five yards deep in the end zone. That was good, but the bad part was that the guy was Gale Sayers. Eleven seconds later the score is 6-0. One minute later Bill Nelson is going to execute our first play and throws the ball with great velocity and character. Unfortunately it went to the Chicago cornerback. It is now 13-0 and our defense has not been on the field yet. But would you believe we won the game 41-13? And the next week we tied the Giants. And so we all went down to the Roosevelt Hotel for cocktails afterward. Hundreds of fans were down there and you'd swear to God we'd won the Super Bowl.

"It was as close as we got to the Super Bowl. We lost the next nine in a row.

"Pittsburgh actually is a great place to play if you want to save money. The Steelers pay average salaries but when I was there you were so ill thought of that you never went out for dinner. You couldn't. You could go to the nicest place in Pittsburgh. People would recognize you as a Steeler and they would come over and start yelling at you. It's the honest to God truth.

"They have tried in some of the media to make a character out of the knuckleball kicker, Booth Lustig. This is too bad, because none of the things they invented about Boots were half as astonishing as the truth. Boots' ball behaved very mysteriously. He is still the only placement kicker in the history of the NFL who kicked a conversion try that went OVER the line and UNDER the goalposts. I mean the ball was higher when it past the line of scrimmage than it was when it past the goal line two yards further.

"He used to start kicking paper cups for practice as soon as our offense got the ball. If every field goal kicker in the league had to kick paper cups, Booth would have made the pro bowl. The trouble was he kicked the paper cups farther than the football.

"He broke up our practice one day and almost turned Ray Mansfield, a fine center, into a soprano. Ray snapped the ball for a field goal attempt, and Dick Hoak — a really great holder — put the ball down. Boots gave it a helluva shot and kicked the ball right into Mansfield's bottom.

"You can imagine the position Mansfield was in, all stretched out like that after just centering the ball. Poor Ray just went down like he took a mortar shot. The whole team was helpless, flopping around the ground laughing, and they carried poor Ray into the locker room.

"The next week Boots kicked Dick Hoak in the hand.

"He just missed the ball completely and hit Hoak square in the knuckles. They said it couldn't be done, but Boots did it.

"Boots had this little blue flight bag in which he carried his shoes. He wore different kinds of shoes for different kicks. Maybe they should have left Boots alone and examined the shoes. We were playing the Eagles, and it had to be the worst pro football game ever played, which is a statement I do not make lightly. That was the famed O. J. Simpson Bowl, in which the loser would get draft rights to O. J.

"Everybody was cheering for us to lose. The Steelers rose to occasion brilliantly and won the game, 6-3 destroying any chance we had of getting O. J. As it turned out, Buffalo was even worse than the Eagles and Steelers and they drafted O. J. But this was the game when Boots put it all together. He had some early discouragements. He missed field goals of 10, 11 and a real toughie of 15 yards — which was right in the middle of the field. The others were off to the side. But with just 10 seconds left and the score tied, in comes Boots

at the 25, and he puts one through. The guys unanimously gave Boots the game ball. It was a tremendous honor because game balls were very rarely given when I was with the Steelers. I mean they were really collector's items. For a while the players debated whether we should give Boots a paper cup instead of a ball.

"But fate, as they say, is no respecter of the mighty. We played a game in Buffalo and got beat by one point. Boots missed a field goal or extra point or some such thing. He felt so bad that he wouldn't even go back on the plane with the team. He grabbed his bags, took a cab and went on the highway hitchhiking.

"And wouldn't you know the guys who picked him up were Buffalo fans, and when they found out who he was they beat the pulp out of him and threw him out. That's the truth. I asked the people in Buffalo about it and they said it happened exactly that way.

"The Steelers had a way of getting people unhinged, not only their fans but the opposing players. I remember Marlin McKeever when he was playing tight end for the Vikings. We were player representatives together so we knew each other pretty well. Marlin went down on a pass against us and was completely wide open. I think Joe Kapp was quarterbacking. Anyhow, it didn't look as though they had a play to Marlin in their game plan. We passed each other a couple of times and he said 'John, they're not covering me.' I said 'that's right,

Marlin, we're not going to cover you all day, because nobody is going to throw to you.' He was really agitated. They ran the same damned play and he must have been open by 20 yards, I swear it. He'd run straight down the middle and he must have been open at least 10 times.

"So McKeever finally said, 'look, I've had it' and just plain walked off the field. He did. He wouldn't play. And that's why they got rid of him at the end of the season.

"What we did to Sonny Jurgensen was a little different. Now this happens to be a great quarterback. In a regular season game he wouldn't have done it, that's for sure. But exhibitions are something else. They don't write your contract on exhibition games. We were playing the Redskins and Jurgensen had gone out for a while. Jim Ninowski was playing quarterback. He came out of the pocket and started running. I caught him about five yards from the sideline and I flat-leveled him. I threw a hook out there and caught him in the throat, and down he went. He didn't move at all. Otto Graham, who was coaching Washington then, came out and I said, 'Otto, I'm sorry. I don't want to hurt him, but I don't want him to run on me.' He said, 'don't worry about it, it's a tough game.'

"They took Jim Ninowski out. As it turns out, he was okay. But right then I figure they were going to start cracking back on me and put my ass out of it. That's what you have to worry about, the blindsiding.

"But Jurgensen came in and in a couple of minutes took the Redskins' mind out of any revenge. It was just as they were taking Ninowski off, and Sonny wasn't real crazy about coming back in. So on this play all of his receivers are covered, and Bill Saul — who is a helluva man and a pretty mean bastard — is the middle linebacker. Sonny has got to scramble. It would be kind of unmanly to do anything else. He's got to run up the middle, which he really doesn't want to do at all.

"He comes through there and Saul comes up on him and I'm moving in from the corner. Sonny is very close to a first down and suddenly he just drops down on his knee and puts the ball up in the air, practically announcing 'HELP! SAVE ME.'

"The crowd starts booing — I remember it was in Norfolk, Va. — and Sonny is just kneeling there, laughing. He could have made the first down if he just dove ahead. In a regular game he would have. But I look over at the sideline and there's Graham, and he's slamming his clipboard on the ground and going out of his gourd.

"Maybe it was just the Steelers. I don't know. We were a pretty scruffy bunch. We used to practice in South Park. We dressed in a first aid station at the old county fair grounds in South Park. It had no windows in the basement. We'd come in and get dressed and brush the snow off our jocks and T-shirts. I'm not kidding. In fact we had an equipment man who would forget now and then that in those quarters you just HAD to shower, a lot. So we took off his clothes one day and burned them right in the middle of the locker room.

"I don't want to give the impression that our men were a bunch of bounders who lacked sophistication.

"But can you imagine Boots Lustig posing for a shaving cream commercial? With some sexy floozy rubbing his cheek to see how smooth it was?"

Better to have the floozy stroking Boots' magic toe — with a paper cup.

Remember to Chart the Restrooms

The electronic wizards who gave America the split-screen and stop-action television admit they have created a dragon.

"There are NFL people who would prefer not to be identified who tell us that more and more customers are belly-aching about seeing better football on TV than they see at the ballpark," one of the wizards laments.

"What they mean is they see more football on TV in any given game. The television playbacks have created an illusion of non-stop action on the screen. The sponsors love it. Years ago, remember what you saw? You saw the official unstacking 5,000 pounds of football players in hope of re-capturing the ball. Then you would see the offensive teams re-arrange itself in the huddle, the camera would come in tight on the right tackle's rear end for 20 seconds, they would break the huddle and dawdle up to the line of scrimmage.

"Has it occurred to you that the only place in America where you can still see that whole, non-violent tableau today is on a football field?

"You cannot see it in your living room anymore. No TV director worth his green pills would consider letting more than two consecutive plays run without isolating the end, freezing the ball-carrier, splitting the tackle or unleashing the color man one-on-one against the cornerback. According to mathematicians the ball is in play only 25 per cent of the time. The rest of the time is devoted to un-piling and the conniving in the huddle. There is also some serious scratching and yelling of hut-hut-hut. With all of its playback stunts, television has just about convinced its watchers that some-thing is always going on.

"Sometimes they get so absorbed in the replay they slop into the live stuff. The modern record was set in the 1971 Super Bowl when Baltimore's John Mackey picked off a pass deflected by the Dallas safetyman and ran for a touchdown. They got it live. They got it from the end zone. They got it in slow motion. They got it on split screen and to top it off they got it from the blimp.

"It was the first time in his life that Unitas made 430 yards on one play.

"The result of all of this is that you have the danger of a developing neurosis among the crowds at live, in-person football games at the stadium.

"Test yourself. How many times did you see a long kickoff return or a fluke play last year and, as if by instinct, settle back to see it again on replay?

"And then you remembered you were at the ball park, and there wasn't going to be a replay.

"And you didn't let on to the guy next to you,

but you sulked just a little bit.

"You have company. Millions of people find themselves in the same boat. There are already a couple of stadium operators, in L. A. and New Orleans, who are planning to put up an instant replay screen ON THE SCOREBOARD.

"There are some technical problems. And they are asking for trouble if they start putting controversial plays up there while the crowd has the officials dead in its sights. But I think you can look for some variation of it spreading to just about every park in the pro league by 1975."

The lack of instant replay is just one of the emotional problems facing the stadium goer in this era of super-glamorization of pro football. The day has disappeared when the fan went to a football game for the simple joy of watching football. You can make a pretty good case for pro football today as adult America's rock festival, although it may trail slightly in riots. I have heard sociologists call it a rejuvenation of the spirit that spawned the French Revolution. And then again it might be America's penance for abandoning the quilting party.

Millions of people now go to a football game seeking an Ultimate Experience. These are the ones against whom you have to take nervy precautions to survive football Sunday at the ball park. Scheming independently, you may already have arrived at some of the more obvious defenses. For those too meek, browbeaten or civilized, I offer a few that have been battle-tested. First, you have to identify the adversary.

1. The transistor radio fanatic. You can recognize this one beneath the stands, long before the kickoff, by his characteristic bearing. Through hundreds of hours of exertions in the stands, he acquired certain structural traits that have permanently altered his features and carriage. He is the man you will see walking down the street with his right hand held up five inches from his ear, his fingers bent claw-like and his head angled at a 30-degree cant, slightly downward.

Often he will nod his head vigorously, as though responding to some fresh outburst of wisdom coming from the general direction of his cupped hand. Once in a while he will shudder. Occasionally he will fling out his left elbow, digging at an imaginary companion to attract his attention.

If you follow him long enough, you may also detect a violent ducking action now and then, giving this strangely-moulded creature the appearance of a man dodging a thrown sausage.

This unusual behavior pattern immediately identifies the transistor nut. It may be a private quirk, but I find him among the most offensive of all the stadium hazards, requiring nothing but the most imaginative and ruthless countermeasures.

I had one sitting three seats away from me for two seasons. Nobody has ever given me a completely acceptable reason why he should not have been strangled, committed or re-located in Baltimore. I am convinced that anybody who listens to the same football game he is watching has a serious and possibly disqualifying problem with equilibrium, in the same league with a man who would make love in a kayak.

It has nothing to do with the quality of the announcers. It does have something to do with fundamental, Bill of Rights-guaranteed, nurtured-in-blood liberties. I have got my binoculars fixed between plays now on the Colts' carnivorous linebacker, Mike Curtis, wondering whether he is planning to tackle the fullback on the next play or swallow him. Don't I have a right to be spared the static-charged exhortation that we should all buy Hamm's beer on the spot? And that what we just saw was the 7th unassisted tackle to go with 14 assists, two saves, and possibly one shutout by Mike Curtis? And also that we should stay tuned for the latest tornado warnings?

You are likely to get all of this, while you are waiting for the next play, and without a pause for punctuation. I don't blame the radio announcers. Dead air is anathema to the radio announcer because it tends to set wrists in motion, changing dials. So we are subjected to a blizzard of information. Much of it is helpful if you are sitting in the front seat of the car. But almost all of it is an annoyance and some of it a by-Christ atrocity if you are sitting in the stands a few yards from the announcer.

The first time I approached the radio freak my manner was the essence of restraint. It was in harmony with the highest democratic principles of equality and live-and-let live. I told him to shut the goddamned thing off so I could enjoy the game in peace.

He might have bought this argument at that, but he never heard me because the volume of the transistor was set in such a way that it could override the combined shrieks, roars and general wall-crumbling of 48,000 people.

Unable to communicate with him vocally, I shifted to the strategy first employed on these shores by the Dutch traders on Manhattan. I tried to bribe him. I showed up for the Viking-49er game with a set of transistor earplugs, which I offered him in the interest of our mutual good health and sanity.

He turned me down, saying he felt isolated from the action if he had to listen to the game without feeling the surge of the crowd. I said I would be happy to provide the surge, a crisp forearm intended to hoist him into the third deck. He said he was sorry if he was irritating me with his transistor radio but he felt naked and uninformed without it. It would be the same, I recall him saying, as listening to the Metropolitan Opera without Milton Cross to distinguish the baritones from the sousaphones.

I never forgot his instructions. The next year I talked a friend into changing seats with me and showed up with my own transistor, which I carried into the seat next to the incumbent freak.

He viewed me with mounting suspicion but remained silent, engraved in the listening position. His right elbow was cocked and his hand clutched at the transistor five inches from his right ear. This made it equidistant from my left ear.

Halfway through the first period, with the suspense suitably high, I turned on my transistor. It was pre-set to one of the local FM stations. In the middle of the Vikings' headlong charge downfield en route to their first field goal, I opened the volume wide.

No announcer invited us to have another Hamm's.

Nobody pinpointed the ball on the 43-1/2 yard line, 18 yards in from the nearest sideline.

Instead, our section was filled with the throbbing chords of the William Tell Overture. It came in full blast just in the movement where all those violins are churning up a big cadenza and you can almost here Brace Beamer shouting "Hi Ho Silver, Awaaaaayyy."

The guy next to me had a better clutch but I had more decibels. The overture soared above the din of the crowd, overpowered his play-by-play announcer and absolutely crushed his station-break man. He had his own set straining right up against red line in power output but there was no way he was going to overtake William Tell. The overture whipped on invincibly, swamping everything in its arpeggios. Toward the end of the timeout the guy began to buckle.

"Okay," he said, "what in blazes is that?"

"It's Rossini," I replied. "What did you expect? Nomellini?"

His mouth was contorted and hugely disdainful. But he was about to submerge. I could tell it. And suddenly William Tell went into that wild, galloping finale which old radio lovers remember as the signal that another Lone Ranger installment was over and you could see the masked man and Tonto heading for the far-off aroyos.

Silence on my radio.

The announcer was saying, "ladies and gentlemen you have just heard Rossini's familiar 'Overture to William Tell.'"

More silence. They were groping for another long-play. Maybe they fell asleep.

The radio nut was counter-attacking again and restored to full stride. It looked like a flop when providentially — as I redialed with no real hope of finding another William Tell — I stumbled upon some Giuseppi Verdi.

This wasn't just any Verdi. I mean it wasn't La Donna Mobile or the quartet from Rigoletto.

What it was, mercifully, was from Il Trovatore and the name of it was The Anvil Chorus.

I hit the top volume lever again. They fell unstoppably on the head of my defenseless neighbor, those mighty blows from a hundred blacksmiths.

He took it for 16 bars.

And then, undramatically, without a sound from

his transistor or his anguished innards, he hung it up. Shut off his radio and sat dumbly watching the action.

The noblest soul is the victor who resists the easy temptation to trample the fallen with lead-footed revenge. I did none of this. I turned my radio down compassionately. Not completely off. I thought the least he deserved was the extended five-day forecasts between the third and fourth quarters.

2. The sky-writing airplane over the stadium. There is a green biplane that has been hauling signs over the stadium in Bloomington for five or six years now. It is slow, noisy, frequently guilty of spelling errors and sometimes endangers high punts.

I have not succeeded yet in shooting down this scroungy commercial parasite but I think I am moving closer to a solution.

My first thought was to get up in a light plane of my own and scatter thousands of tin foil strips into the circling pattern of the boisterous biplane. This is nothing more than the standard technique for jamming radar. The idea was not necessarily to send the plane down in flames but merely to clog its propellor a little, reducing its airspeed. This in turn would force it into making a harmless crash landing in the river bottoms.

I also considered 4th of July-style exploding rockets and the so-called "smart" box kites that can home in on all objects below 3,000 feet.

Both of these showed promise. They had to be rejected when an attorney pointed out they were in violation of the Geneva Accords protecting combatants against inhumane instruments of war.

The solution I am proposing is the release of thousands of helium-filled toy balloons as the plane approaches the stadium airspace.

I decided on this defense after recalling the experience years ago of one Judge Eugene Minenko, a World War II pilot who for a time flew with the Civil Air Patrol in the post-war period. To stay current and on active status, the judge was required to log a certain number of solo hours in the CAP's light observation planes.

The judge one autumn chose a Saturday afternoon to meet these requirements. He was frolicking high over St. Paul when he noticed a large cluster of balloons floating on a southeasterly heading. The judge instantly remembered it was homecoming day at the University of Minnesota and the balloons no doubt were launched from Memorial Stadium in Minneapolis.

Lacking other available targets, the old dogfighter put his little craft in a tight bank and came up on the balloons from 4 o'clock, directly out of the sun. The balloons were taken by surprise and offered scant resistance.

With great zeal, the judge charged into the thin-skinned globes, happily stabbing them by the score with his whirling propellor.

The balloons were dispatched with no losses to

our side. The judge broke off the engagement and resumed his altitude.

Five minutes later the plane began yawing and bucking and carrying on something fierce. The judge checked the controls but found all systems in order. He scanned out the window at the ailerons and the flaps, and detected nothing. Then he looked behind him, and groaned in dismay.

Tethered to the tail assembly were 500 balloons — red balloons, blue balloons and balloons imploring the finder to "Skindiana."

The judge reacted as though blindsided by a Messerschmitt. He slipped and banked and Immelmanned and dived. He was never sure whether the balloons were lifting him up or dragging him down, but he knew one thing for sure: They had shot the hell out all of the plane's aerodynamics. There were all in a bunch, a second cluster that had ambushed the judge while he was busy deflating the first.

It took him 15 minutes and all of the aerobatics the plane could perform to dislodge the gaseous hitchhikers.

To this day the judge will not go near a circus.

I offer this as a word to the wise to all skywriting pilots planning to work the stadium circuit this fall.

3. The restroom hogs. Rest room facilities are limited at many stadia. The situation is complicated in some arenas where tailgating is practiced on a large scale. At Metropolitan Stadium in Bloomington, for instance, the stadium manage-

ment has consistently ignored the most pitiable cries by the multitudes for outdoor biffy service. They have counseled, instead, the virtues of restraint and discipline. This in turn has spawned a race of Minnesota football goers identified by their grimly clenched teeth, gnawed gums and crossed legs.

It is axiomatic that you have to be tough to watch a football game in Minnesota.

It also helps to be a skilled actor. Hundreds have avoided the ultimate embarrassment by walking about with small laboratory beakers. They explain to the curious that their examining doctor keeps Sunday hours and has asked for the usual little vials now to beat the Monday rush.

Competition for places in the restroom line at halftime is frequently vicious and sometimes devoid of the most common chivalries. There have been cases where some of the standees, driven to the final extremities, have tried to intimidate those in front of them with threats so horrifying they absolutely cannot be repeated here.

Only the most haphazard fan goes to a football game under such circumstances without a basic floor plan of the stadium. The important thing is to keep your options open. Know the location of johns by deck and section. Know the consumption habits of the various sections. It may surprise you that these may differ radically. You may find one section especially partial to popcorn, which is a section you will want to angle toward a few minutes before halftime. Another may be partial to beer, which is a section you will scrupulously avoid.

Under all conditions, try not to be boorish or selfish. The rallying cry of the oppressed is to help your neighbor. Like anything else, of course, even in restroom manners, there are limits.

4. Know-it-all neighbors in the stands. A universal menace, but one easily silenced. The weapon here is the tape recorder. One of my friends tried it four years ago when Joe Kapp and Gary Cuozzo were quarterbacking the Vikings. In the seat directly in front of him was a bulky man with a pumpkin face and a voice penetrating enough to announce air raids. Pumpkin hated quarterbacks. It didn't matter what they were named. If they did not complete 25 consecutive passes every week they were clowns, plumbers and cursed of God.

In mid-season one game Pumpkin stood up and screamed, "Cuozzo, you got an arm like a rusty beer sign. Sit down for somebody who knows how. All right, Grant. Get Kapp in there. All you're gonna get from Cuozzo is beat."

My buddy quietly pulled a Webcor tape recorder out of his quilted footbag, put it up against Pumpkin's porkpie hat and turned it to "play."

The voice was unmistakeably Pumpkin's, recorded one week before. It carried 15 rows up into the third deck. "Kapp," it screamed, "you got an arm like a rusty beer sign. Get out of there and make room for somebody who can pass. Everything you throw looks like a shot goose. Grant, get Kapp out of there. All he's gonna get you is beat."

Pumpkin shriveled noticeably.

He didn't open his mouth again until the next play.

Could Francis Have Been a
Master Criminal?

Football is the stuff of legends. For decades it was simply understood that Knute Rockne got the idea for the Notre Dame shift by watching the chorus line at the Roxy Theater.

Later, more scholarly research uncovered the fact that Rock actually stumbled into the shift when a sophomore halfback from Kalamazoo had trouble counting to three. He kept jumping the quarterback's count and bungled Rockne into a dynasty.

The trouble with legends is the congestion they foist on the gullible. They tend to pile up. You have to sort out the ones that are clearly fraudulent from the ones that are merely under suspicion.

In following football, it is wise to hold your myths to the lowest possible workable figure. For this reason I have assembled the most popular. These you are free to discard, or to embrace with even greater ferocity, depending on your level of sentimentality. In each case, however, the original thesis behind the myth has long since been pretty well blown up. I am sorry, but that is how it is.

I will take the current arbor of myths in order of

their hardiness.

1. The object of the game is to score a touchdown.

This proposition has been in doubt for some time now but was disproved convincingly in 1971. The object of the game, plainly, is to kick a field goal.

There was a time when the touchdown was one of the symbols of man's fulfillment here on earth. It was the mountain scaled, the chasm bridged, the mortgage paid. Men sacrificed and schemed for it and women, at least the more devoted camp followers, surrendered their last vestiges of virtue for it.

At pro football's present pace, the touchdown is headed for eventual enshrinement in the Hall of Fame at Canton, Ohio as an artifact of a vanished age.

What has deflowered the old touchdown is the evangelistic passion for defense in modern football. Most teams now subscribe to the idea that nobody can hurt them as long as their own offense stays off the field.

As a result the idols of the masses no longer are the Luckmans and Baughs and Jimmy Browns but leviathans like Alan Page, Bob Lilly, Carl Eller and Dick Butkus. You used to be able to incite thousands by yelling "touchdown, touchdown." Today you yell "DE-fense, DE-fense, DE-fense." You yell it whether the defense is on the field or not. There was a day two years ago at Metropolitan Stadium when a sizeable number of Viking parishioners booed Detroit's decision to punt from midfield. It meant the Viking defense had to retire to the bench, thus forfeiting a possible interception or fumble recovery — easily the team's most powerful scoring threat that season.

So now you will notice the field goal kicker begin to twitch whenever his team goes onto the attack. Acquiring yardage is easy cheese from the offensive team's 20 to the defense's 40. Once beyond midfield, though, the offense begins to make gestures of alarm. It has a sense of being on forbidden ground. Terror begins to seize the invading athletes, much as it did the sailors of Columbus. The parallel is closer than you think. Both were afraid of falling off the edge. Thus you will see the typical pro football, once it crosses the 50, design its next play with the primary intent of avoiding a fumble. The next one is intended to avoid an intercepted pass. The third moves the ball into the middle of the field and the fourth is a field goal attempt. There is rarely a deviation.

You can tell your friends the sequence the next time you're at the ball park. It will prepare them for the final score, 12-9.

2. God is on the side of the team with the biggest tackles.

Variations of this have been with us for decades. The basic premise is now under challenge, since there is some dispute about the recent piety of big tackles.

God now appears to be on the side of the team with the fewest number of linebackers playing out their options.

3. Francis Tarkenton has reformed and is now a drop-back quarterback.

This allegation has been made with the regularity of the tide since the cool-eyed squire from Georgia first arrived in pro football. Occasionally Francis will play a game in which the whole universe suddenly falls into harmony, the planets are in their proper orbits and he does not scramble one time. Like the passage of Haley's comet, such a game recurs 75 years later.

With only the faintest arch of the eyebrow, Francis insists that he never really was a scrambler in his soul — that his bizarre conduct was forced on him in his formative years by primitive linemen who came at him with harmful intent and very little resistance.

Enemy linebackers have another theory. "There's no question that Francis was born with renegade, unorthodox tendencies," maintains one of them, a winded pursuer of Tarkenton from the early days. "I'm amazed he didn't become a master criminal. If he went into baseball it wouldn't have been more than three years when he was running the bases from third to second to first.

"I never did buy this business about Francis The New Conformist. They pinned that label on him the first time in 1963 and the next week the Vikings went to Green Bay. They got into clutch situation and Francis went back to pass. Flatley, his main receiver, was supposed to sprint straight down the field. But he knew Francis better than any of us and he came off the line like he was starting out on the 10,000 meter run.

"I think Francis had every intention of throwing the ball on his third loop across the field. By this time he was 25 yards behind the line of scrimmage, which we usually figured was about ideal for Francis' peace of mind. But he was really off on a bender this time. On his fourth swing across the field he started waving to Flatley. Then he waved to Gordy Smith. They waved back. Pretty soon the Packer defensive backs were picking it up, and they were waving, too. By the time he came across the field the fifth time, 10,000 people in the crowd were waving. You didn't know how the hell he was going to pick out a receiver from that mess.

"The thing is, when Tarkenton waves once it means the receiver should run another 15 yards, cut between the tarpaulin and Gate 5, and come back toward the goal posts.

"He waved five times to Flatley. That is the maximum-emergency wave. Flatley told me himself later he had already run north, east, west and south and the only place left was the Fox River.

"So Flatley kept running until he couldn't run anymore and he just fell to the ground, exhausted. Three Packer defensive linemen were in the same position 50 yards upfield, stiff and horizontal. The only guy still chasing Tarkenton was Willie Davis, and it looked like Willie was starting to stumble, first over the yard-lines and then over his tongue.

"Well, Tarkenton just stopped and threw that ball toward the end of the stadium. How's that for pinpoint control? The ball went 35 yards and then fell for lack of speed. I don't have to tell you where it ended up. It went right to Flatley, lying there on the ground. Flatley was too tired to argue. He didn't even put up his hands. The ball landed on his gut, bounced twice and came to rest in the crook of his arm. They called it complete and a first down. They tell me Lombardi damned near fainted. He lifted his head to the sky and for awhile Van Brocklin was afraid Vince was going to turn Tarkenton into a frog. He had the power, you know. Four years later Van Brocklin wanted to know why he didn't.

"People ask me what you need to stop Tarkenton. I tell them the Lord's Prayer and a recession. I'm not trying to be funny. Besides being a first-rate football player he really complicates life for the defensive player. He puts the linebacker in what we call a bastard position. First, you've got to drop back to protect your area on a pass. When he starts running, you don't know what to do because there's no defense in pro football coordinated to stop a running quarterback. I mean there's really no man assigned to him. This is why linebackers love to take a good shot at the quarterback. The idea is to change his mind a little about running. But Tarkenton reads that sideline like a fortune teller reads tea leaves. You almost never get a good whack at him. I know he's got a new team again and they say he's suddenly going to be a classic quarterback. Did Rumplestiltskin give up tricks? The urge to scramble is like insanity in the family. You don't know when it's going to crop up. But it will, at the most embarrassing times for linebackers."

Bring on the men in the little white jackets.

4. Football coaches are stolid creatures, almost inaccessible to the fan off the field.

Let me share with you the small but winsome encounter between Forrest D. Johnson, football fan from Fargo, N. D., and Norman Van Brocklin, turbulent football coach and a wary man at the bar.

"We got to be regulars at the Viking summer practices in Bemidji," Mr. Johnson tells us. "An additional flavor of expectancy in 1964 was a bull of a halfback by the name of Dave Osborn, a North Dakotan who was trying to make the squad.

"One night at Jack's Supper Club on the highway I spied the Dutchman halfway across the room relaxing with this coaching staff over a few beers.

"My first thought was to personally plug for Osborn. Clearer heads prevailed. So I wrote the following note on a cocktail napkin, and dispatched it by waitress to the coaches' table:

"'Keep Osborn — North Dakota Needs the Publicity.'"

"When the waitress placed my message in front of him, my ego was immediately destroyed because

LEGENDS

he gave it only a cursory look, and then tossed it aside.

"But hark! Second thoughts. He retrieved the sodden napkin, borrowed a pen from Harry Gilmer, scribbled something that I knew had to be profound, and gave it back to the waitress.

"I practically tore it from her grasp when she got to the table.

"It read:

"'Why would anyone from North Dakota want publicity!'"

"So, it made you sort of love the guy, right? I mean all that wit? I waved to him and he waved back. The next day I met a couple of the sports writers and was introduced to a couple of owners. On my way back to the stands I passed Van Brocklin. He was working with his backs. He glanced at me and said, 'hey fella, get your ass back up in the stands.'"

The moral is, at football practices get everything back into the stands quickly and if the coach is Van Brocklin, do it even more so.

5. There is a certain comradeship among rival players on the field. Reports that players sometimes will try to "get" an opponent are pulp magazine stuff.

We will allow the winded, retired linebacker to resume the podium.

"Nobody tells you to play dirty, you understand. It happens subconsciously. I've had people say 'when some guy on the other team is limping and you know this game is bread and butter, don't you try to soften the blow a little?'

"Yeah, we do, so little you can't really tell it. What you do if you know the guy has a bad knee is maybe send two or three guys at him in hopes that you might, well, aggravate it a little bit, as the doctors put it. You don't really want to put the guy out for the season. That's a libel, really. All you want to do is put him out for the game.

"Another thing I've heard is that pro football teams don't gang up on the bad guys anymore. Ask your buddy Pellington of Baltimore. He was having a happy time calling Tommy Mason all kinds of names one game and threatening to turn his skin into a lampshade. He got a little rougher than that. So on three straight plays our guys just forgot the play and put the wood to Pelly, six at a time. They carried him away on the third play.

"He was back the next time Baltimore was on defense, wearing two splints and eight stitches. To this day Mason insists the Vikings had the craziest backfield in the league the rest of the game — one quarterback, one fullback, one flanker and one lampshade."

6. The competitive urge is what draws athletes to a league like the NFL.

Romanticists might be willing to live with this one, but a very large rebuttal to it is Mick Tingelhoff, the best center in pro football for 10 years. Although not drafted by the Vikings, Tingelhoff was actively courted by both the Vikings and the American Football League. The Vikings brought Mick into Chicago after his senior season at Nebraska, to witness the Viking-Bear game and to see first-hand some of the sacrifices demanded of the pro footballer. Among these was Saturday night dinner with Stan West, a coaching assistant and a professional Lusty Oklahoman. The sacrifice entailed listening to West's barnyard epics. West had more finesse than the surface signs indicated. His personal responsibility was to sign Tingelhoff at all costs. Toward that end, Stan arranged to have the table serviced by the bustiest, most deeply-cleft blonde on the Sheraton-Chicago's staff.

Tingelhoff was a son of the sodhouses, highly impressionable in the city. West ordered him a beer. Tingelhoff was impressed. It was served by the bulbous blonde. Tingelhoff was even more urgently impressed. Each time West would order another beer, the blonde's bosom would approach the table from a lower horizon. On the fifth one the blonde's great swelling bounty finally succumbed to the laws of gravity and burst free of all restraining fabric.

Recovering splendidly, she handed Tingelhoff his glass of beer, rumpled his hair and left in flowing billows.

West gently removed the untouched beer glass from the stricken rookie's hand. Unobtrusively, he replaced it with a ballpoint pen.

"There is nothin' like the NFL, Mick, baby,"

he said. "We need young, dedicated, tough-fibered young men like you in this here league."

Tingelhoff was the only player in the NFL to sign in 1961 with an open mouth and marbled eyes.

7. The advertisers have gone about as far as they can go milking pro football.

This is dangerous wishful thinking, according to one of the advertising trade's most brazen innovaters, Allen N. Fahden.

"We have still not seen the ultimate in sports endorsements," Mr. Fahden contends. "I see a dozen executives sitting along a table and the account executive produces a glittering white smile to announce (a) the agency's tooth paste campaign is still doing fabulously well and (b) it has pulled off a major coup.

"'We have done it,' he says, 'we have signed for exclusive rights to all of the jerseys in pro football as a new advertising medium. There will be a word or words on the back of each. They will be so aligned as to spell out a message in the style of the Burma Shave road signs.

"'Yes, I know we will get greater visibility on the back of a giant lineman than we will on the back of a 118-pound field goal kicker from Yogoslavia. But that will be part of the new art, you understand, fitting the message to the surface. I also understand the problem with tearaway jerseys endangering a multi-million dollar campaign. These can be overcome. Our media dollar is buying the huddle and all offensive and defensive formations except the

162

prevent and gap 8.

"'Naturally, our best stuff will be reserved for the huddle. We have a degree of control there. But we also figure to do some good, abbreviated messages on the three-man rush. Eller, Page, and Marshall will be so aligned as to spell out World's Fastest Lather!

"'I know you will ask, gentlemen, how to keep the words in the right order. There is really no stress there. The agency will be calling the plays. We'll be on the headphones at all times calling down copy changes to the coach. Free substitution gives us the right to rewrite-in a stronger verb without as much as a timeout or a feigned injury.

"'We've even got the coaches to agree to punt on first and goal to go if we run out of copy for the offensive team's series of plays.'"

We are not so far from the last days of Rome as you may have imagined.

8. Football is approaching the saturation level on television.

This is the doomsday prophecy that has been made annually since 1962. Since then, the first year of football's predicted demise on TV, the pro leagues have made something like $200 million on television, the players salaries have climbed past $100,000, the number of neurotic women has trebled and the incidence of astigmatism among men has quadrupled. By the year 2,000 the NFL headquarters will acquire the Pentagon for new office space, Joe Namath will buy J. Paul Getty's art collection and America will awake at 7 o'clock each Monday morning to the familiar sound:

"Well, Dandy, we're all set for the kickoff of the weekly Football at Dawn and I've got to tell you who I just had breakfast with . . ."